THE WANDERING JEW

by Michelene Wandor and Mike Alfreds
adapted from Eugene Sue's French classic

A METHUEN PAPERBACK

WHAT HAPPENS NEXT

In 1985, Ian McKellen and Edward Petherbridge invited me to direct a production for their group at the National Theatre. My brief was to find some material which would accommodate the whole company. I think they were hoping I would create a piece of narrative theatre, a genre with which some of my previous work had identified me. I read over a hundred plays and novels and met some of the company to find out what material would interest them. I was bombarded with titles and ideas. Among them was a suggestion by Nichola McAuliffe of a novel she remembered from her father's bookshelf, a nineteenth-century epic filled with character and incident. I dutifully added it to my lengthening book list and went home to continue reading *The Tale of Genji*. Eventually her recommendation came to the top of the pile and I was confronted by five hundred large pages in double-columns and minute print. I heaved the volume onto my desk, focused a strong light over it and, at risk to eyesight, I embarked on Eugene Sue's *The Wandering Jew*. From the first page (a mysterious encounter across the Bering Strait during the aurora borealis) I was gripped by the narrative. If the book hadn't been too heavy to hold, I couldn't have put it down. During the ten days it took me to read it, I grew more and more certain that this was what I wanted to do.

Periodically, I have been wrapped over the knuckles when I have chosen to stage novels rather than plays. My immediate reaction was that I found them (more) theatrical and (more) dramatic. When I considered more thoughtfully what it was that attracted me to certain novels, it was because they contained characters vibrantly in action. Nineteenth-century novelists, especially, seem to have been in part frustrated dramatists. In the absence of a serious theatre, they poured their sense of the dramatic into their books. They wrote scene after stunning scene of conflict, revelation, reunion, separation. Meticulously detailed descriptions of body language heighten this sense of performance. Frequently, one comes across such phrases as 'the actors in this scene . . .' But, above all, the characters seem to demand to be put on stage: innumerable characters in search of an adaptor.

A lot of contemporary theatre has removed itself from narrative and linear sequence. I am suspicious of the cult of 'image' in fashionable theatre. Imagery tends to be private and static, qualities not immediately associated with theatre. Plot, however, is public and active. It is public because it controls the manner of its own unfolding, its speed and its duration; the whole audience has to experience it simultaneously. The reader and viewer, on the other hand, can control their contact with a novel or a painting. They stop, turn away, re-read, slow down, speed up as they feel inclined. And plot is active because it is, in fact, the sum of all the internal and external actions that the characters pursue in the course of their story.

The Wandering Jew has a wonderful and abundant plot. I never did direct it for the McKellen-Petherbridge company. It remained unfinished business until my own company at the National provided me with the opportunity to stage it. So two years later I offer the production as a tribute to Plot and as an acknowledgement of our need to know what happens next.

Mike Alfreds, 1987

INTRODUCTION

Eugene Sue was born in 1804, into a wealthy family. He became a naval physician, and in 1830 began to write fiction. He is reputed to have produced the first really popular literature in France, with a readership that straddled different social classes.

The Wandering Jew (*Le Juif Errant*) was serialised in a French periodical from June 1844 to July 1845; English translators stood by, quills at the ready, and almost simultaneously with the French publication nine versions were published in London.

I knew of the legend of the Wandering Jew (a Christian story about a man condemned to wander till the day of judgement for having rebuffed Christ on the way to the crucifixion), and I knew of the existence of the novel, before Mike Alfreds approached me. Like many nineteenth-century blockbusters, it is a fascinating nightmare to read. It has everything in it, bar the proverbial kitchen sink – and that is probably because the poor, about whom Sue wrote, did not have plumbed in running water, and hence no kitchen sink.

The novel is a hybrid text; because it was written for serial publication, Sue himself often didn't know what turn the story would take. The book is full of blind plot-alleys and repetitions (needed to bring the story up to date for new readers). The dialogue is overblown, hothouse rhetoric (serial writers were often paid by the page), alongside passages of wonderful description (the pre-camera strength of nineteenth-century prose), journalistic polemic on the working conditions of the poor, and religious tract material. Buried in this haystack of a book is actually a simple story which can be described in a single sentence. It is the manner of its unfolding that is fascinating, and the challenge of making a coherent dramatic out of such a complex and contradictory text.

The story unrolls more in the style of a fairy tale or an opera than a social realist tale. It draws on the potent images and conventions of its time, combining the gothic novel, the adventure story, anguished, semi-pornographic sexuality, romance and innocent faith. At one level, the sheer apparent impossibility of the project was what appealed to me most. The question boiled down to the simple one of how to find a theatrical form and a language that retained the heightened melodramatic spirit of the original, and yet would still appeal to a modern audience.

I love working with texts; dramatising, adapting, translating, transforming. All these terms are appropriate for the complex process that produces a new text, true to the spirit of the original, even if it sometimes deviates from the letter. Dramatising involves entering into a dialogue with the original text, finding the clues in it that will lead to new solutions. This play is an event in its own right, even though its essential correspondence with the parent text is close throughout. The novelish feature of evocative description is retained in the convention of the 'open lines', which can function either as spoken narrative, or as stage direction, or simply smooth the reading of the text without necessarily being spoken in performance.

From a practical point of view, Mike Alfreds and I had a number of meetings during the summer of 1986 to discuss the book and possible ways of staging it. I then wrote the play, and we discussed each draft. In the event, he made the final decisions vis-à-vis the version in performance, and I have made the final decisions vis-à-vis the published text, but I am responsible for both texts.

Michelene Wandor, 1987

The Wandering Jew was first performed at the National Theatre, London on 8 August 1987. The cast was as follows:

IGNATIUS MOROK	James Smith	MAGISTRATE	Brian Badcoe
LA MORT	Richard Hahlo	JACQUES RENNEPONT, *called Couche-*	
GOLIATH	Metin Marlow	*Tout-Nu*	Nick Dunning
DAGOBERT BAUDOIN	Russell Enoch	ROSE POMPON	Kate Godfrey
JOVIAL	Nick Dunning	CEPHYSE, *called Queen of the Revels*	
BLANCHE SIMON	Kate Godfrey		Sylvestra Le Touzel
ROSE SIMON	Sylvestra Le Touzel	MOTHER SUPERIOR	Andrée Evans
JOSEPH	Pip Donaghy	BATHSHEBA SAMUEL	Andrée Evans
EVA	Maggie Wells	DAVID SAMUEL	Brian Badcoe
MARSHAL SIMON	Brian Badcoe	NOTARY	Pip Donaghy
BURGOMASTER	Brian Badcoe	MARIUS DE RENNEPONT	Nick
PRINCE DJALMA	Mark Rylance		Dunning
THE STRANGLER	Metin Marlow	NURSE	Paola Dionisotti
JOSHUA VAN DAEL	Nick Dunning	CARDINAL MALIPIERI	Andrée Evans
FARINGHEA	Pip Donaghy	FIRST PRIEST	Nick Dunning
RODIN	Philip Voss	SECOND PRIEST	Richard Hahlo
ABBE D'AIGRIGNY	James Smith	THIRD PRIEST	Metin Marlow
HERODIAS	Paola Dionisotti	FIRST HOSPITAL ORDERLY	Metin
1ST SPY	Richard Hahlo		Marlow
2ND SPY	Metin Marlow	SECOND HOSPITAL ORDERLY	
FRANCOISE BAUDOIN	Paola		Richard Hahlo
	Dionisotti	GRAVEDIGGER	Metin Marlow
MAGDALENE SOLIVEAU, *called La*		FATHER CABOCCINI	Lucien Taylor
Mayeux	Maggie Wells	NARRATION BY	The Company
AGRICOLA BAUDOIN	Mark Rylance		
ABBE GABRIEL	Lucien Taylor	*Musicians*	
MME AUGUSTINE GRIVOIS	Andrée	Claire van Kampen	*(piano/music director)*
	Evans	Rory Allam	*(synthesiser)*
GEORGETTE	Susanna Bishop	Timothy Caister	*(horn)*
ADRIENNE DE CARDOVILLE	Sian	Nicholas Hayley	*(violin)*
	Thomas	Andrea Hess	*(cello)*
FLORINE	Sylestra Le Touzel	Neil Rowland	*(percussion)*
PRINCESS DE ST DIZIER	Paola	Rebecca Wexler	*(viola)*
	Dionisotti		
SCRIBE	Metin Marlow	*Director*	Mike Alfreds
DOCTOR BALEINIER	Pip Donaghy	*Design and Lighting*	Paul Dart
CONFESSOR	Russell Enoch	*Music*	Ilona Sekacz
POLICEMAN	Richard Hahlo	*Music Direction*	Claire van Kampen

Prologue

dark

cold

eternal ice

two cold worlds

Siberia

North America

empty   cold   wind   cold   snow   empty   cold

footsteps

small, light feet

large, deep footprints

impressions on the hard, polished snow

birds

rustling

flying

night birds   sweeping   dismayed

A half globe of intense brilliance on the horizon

from its centre, columns of light

illuminate the sky

the earth

the sea

rays, vivid as fire

spread over the desert snows

the icebergs turn purple

the high black rocks turn red

the aurora borealis

between the Arctic ocean and the Bering sea, two continents meet

facing one another across the Bering Straits

HERODIAS: On the Siberian cape, a man stretches his arms towards America

JOSEPH: On the American promontory, a woman points to heaven

PART ONE

Scene 1

The Inn of the White Falcon, near Leipzig.

The middle of October, 1831.

A vast loft.

Lit by a copper lamp.

A stove, charcoal piled ready.

Iron chains, spiked collars, traps with teeth like saws, muzzles bristling with nails.

Rosaries. Vases for holy water. The framed images of saints.

Pamphlets telling of modern miracles; terrible predictions for the years 1831 and 1832, directed against impious and revolutionary France.

An autographed letter from the Saviour to one of the faithful.

Ignatius Morok, Siberian hunter, converted and baptised in the Catholic faith.

Prominent cheekbones.

Long pale beard.

Dull yellow hair falls straight to his shoulders.

He is wrapped in a blood-red cloak, lined with black fur.

Tamer of wild beasts.

Evangelist.

Showman.

Goliath climbs into the loft.

A low forehead.

Coarse hair and beard.

Dust on his clothes.

MOROK: Thou hast met them?

GOLIATH: Yesterday.

MOROK: God be praised.

GOLIATH: A white horse. Two young girls in mourning. An old man with a long moustache.

MOROK: Didst get the old man to talk?

GOLIATH: No. He is a surly creature, strong and resolute, though little more than skin and bone. I advise you, master, take care.

MOROK: As I tamed the panther, so I will break the old man.

GOLIATH: You will never make a lamb out of this old wolf.

MOROK: I have faith. Thou hast done well, Goliath.

GOLIATH: Thank you, master. Now I must attend to the beasts' supper.

MOROK: Thou wilt not feed the beasts this evening.

GOLIATH: But master –

MOROK: I forbid thee to feed them. Thou canst eat.

GOLIATH: I never eat without my beasts.

MOROK: If thou dare'st feed them, I will turn thee away.

GOLIATH: Come, master, only poor La Mort, just a morsel to satisfy her.

MOROK: It is the panther above all I forbid thee to feed.

GOLIATH: But why?

MOROK: Heat the iron bar in the stove.

GOLIATH: But Master –

MOROK: And there will be ten florins for thee.

GOLIATH: Very well, Master.

Scene 2

A serene sky.

Tall reeds bend their velvet heads beneath a light breeze.

The sun gradually disappears behind purple clouds tipped with flame.

An old Napoleonic warrior. Dagobert Baudoin.

He leads an old white horse, battle-scarred like himself.

Two girls are seated on the horse.

Twins.

Fifteen years old.

Rose and Blanche Simon.

Rose's sweet face shows beneath a black velvet hood, from which escapes a profusion of light chestnut ringlets.

A profusion of light chestnut ringlets frames Blanche's rosy cheeks.

Rose's lips are like a carnation damp with dew.

Blanche's eyes are as blue as forget-me-nots.

Their hearts beat in unison.

ROSE: Where are we?

BLANCHE: Why have we stopped?

DAGOBERT: My dear children. Eighteen years ago this very day, on the eve of the battle of Leipzig, I carried your wounded father to this oak tree. Here he and I were taken prisoner. Come, you must not weep. Remember that your mother watches over you from heaven. Do not grieve her by crying.

ROSE: Thou art right, Dagobert.

BLANCHE: We will not cry any more.

DAGOBERT: Hast thou the medal she gave thee?

ROSE: What does it mean? 'Victim of The Company. Pray for me. Paris, 13th February, 1682.'

BLANCHE: 'Be at No 3 Rue St Francois, Paris, on the 13th February, 1832. Pray for me.'

ROSE: What does it mean, Dagobert?

DAGOBERT: I will tell you tonight, at the Inn of the White Falcon. Come. It is growing dark. We must hurry.

Scene 3

The Courtyard of the White Falcon Inn.

MOROK: At last.

Morok sees two girls taken to their room.

He sees a horse led to the stable.

He sees an old man with a tub.

By the light of a lantern, he is washing clothes.

He rubs away at a handkerchief spread on a plank.

MOROK: A washerwoman with a grey moustache. It would seem, comrade, you have not much confidence in the German

washerwomen. I do believe you are French, my dear fellow. An old soldier of the empire, perhaps. A hero, wearing petticoats? Are you deaf and dumb, sir?

DAGOBERT: I do not know you. I do not wish to know you. Leave me alone.

MOROK: I always enjoy meeting Frenchmen abroad, particularly when they can wield the soap as well as you do. If I had a housekeeper, I'd send her to you for lessons. You are not polite, my General of the suds. I knew that Napoleon's soldiers were pagans who stabled their horses in church. But I did not know they were cowards. This man has insulted me. And I require an apology. Or he will give me satisfaction.

What, fight?

You'll get yourselves arrested.

There are laws against duelling.

The burgomaster will put you in prison.

MOROK: Who will inform against us?

No, no, no.

Not us.

Do as you like.

Just a bit of friendly advice.

MOROK: The Lord commands us to protect His honour. So. A Napoleonic soldier has become a washerwoman and a coward?

DAGOBERT: I refuse to fight.

Scene 4

In the stable

Dagobert's horse, Jovial.

He strains at his halter.

A cold sweat speckles his hide.

Scene 5

Rose and Blanche's room.

On the table near the window is Dagobert's knapsack and a single lamp.

BLANCHE: Dost thou think Gabriel will come again tonight?

ROSE: Oh yes, he promised.

BLANCHE: Our guardian angel.

ROSE: Sent by our mother.

BLANCHE: He is so handsome.

ROSE: It is fortunate that he loves us both.

BLANCHE: How could he love Blanche without loving Rose?

ROSE: Perhaps we shall dream of him again in Paris. Think, Blanche, how beautiful it must be.

BLANCHE: A city of gold.

ROSE: A city where everyone is happy, and good.

A loud crash.

BLANCHE: What is that?

ROSE: The window is broken.

BLANCHE: Oh, Dagobert!

DAGOBERT: What is wrong?

ROSE: We did not recognise thy footsteps.

BLANCHE: We were talking and we heard a great crash.

DAGOBERT: The wind must have blown the shutter loose. Fear not, it was only the wind.

BLANCHE: Where hast thou been?

ROSE: Thou art pale. Is anything wrong?

DAGOBERT: No. Nothing. Now, children, I must talk to you. You know that your father was a working man, who enlisted as a private soldier and became a Marshal of France. At the battle of Leipzig he and I were taken prisoner by a Frenchman, a Colonel d'Aigrigny who betrayed France by going over to fight in the Russian army against the French. We were taken to Warsaw, and there the General first met and fell in love with your mother, Eva. In 1814 the war ended, and the Emperor was banished to the island of Elba. Your father joined him, and when war broke out again, children, your father fought like a lion. After the battle, the Emperor, to the joy of the whole army, made your father a Duke and Marshal of France.

BLANCHE: Is that the Emperor's portrait on thy silver cross?

DAGOBERT: He pinned it on me with his own hands. But then came Waterloo, a day of great sadness, when old soldiers like myself wept. The English carried the Emperor to St Helena, another island at the end of the world. The Marshal was part of a conspiracy to free him, but he was found out. Your father again met that traitor d'Aigrigny and defeated him in a duel, after which the Marshal fled back to Warsaw. You mother had waited for him and they were married.

BLANCHE: Were they happy?

DAGOBERT: Very happy. But there was much to grieve them. The Russians again began to treat the Poles as their slaves. Your brave mother spoke out boldly where others dared not. She was sent to Siberia, some months before you were born. I accompanied her with Jovial. Thus it was, with her on horseback, and I leading her then as I lead you now, that we arrived in the village where you were born.

ROSE: And our father?

DAGOBERT: He was banished from all the Russian Dominions. I did not hear from him again until the day your poor mother died.

BLANCHE: We went to the pine forest that day.

ROSE: To fetch some heather for her.

DAGOBERT: As I worked in the garden, I heard a voice.

JOSEPH: Is this the village of Milosk?

DAGOBERT: I saw a stranger.

JOSEPH: Does Madame Simon live here?

DAGOBERT: She does, sir.

JOSEPH: I have travelled from Warsaw to find her. I have news from Marshal Simon. He is in India.

EVA: Dagobert, I have a letter from the General.

DAGOBERT: Your father had sent her his journal. It is in my knapsack, with my cross and our papers.

BLANCHE: Oh, may we read it?

ROSE: Please, Dagobert.

DAGOBERT: Of course you may.

BLANCHE: My beloved Eva. What has become of you? How I miss you – and our child. He must be fourteen now. Whom does he resemble?

SIMON: We have beaten the English and forced them out of this part of India, which they invaded in contempt of all justice.

EVA: Yesterday I received a letter from Paris. I have good news for Dagobert. His son, Agricola, has a new job in a factory, where he wields the heavy forge hammer as if it were a feather. When he returns home to his mother to whom he is devoted, he writes patriotic verses, poetry full of fire and energy.

DAGOBERT: It pleases me that he is good to his mother.

SIMON: Gabriel, an orphan whom Dagobert's wife adopted some years ago, is very different.

ROSE:
BLANCHE: Gabriel?

ROSE: Is he handsome?

SIMON: Gabriel is as thoughtful and quiet as Agricola is lively and active. He is very devout, angelic, even. One of the Brothers at his church school spoke of him to a person of consequence, and Gabriel has become a priest.

DAGOBERT: I have no time for priests.

ROSE: Perhaps he is a good priest?

BLANCHE: He must be a good man if he is called Gabriel.

EVA: He has devoted himself to foreign missions, and has set out for America.

SIMON: Adieu, my beloved Eva. Clasp our child to your bosom and cover it with all the kisses I send you from the depths of exile.

ROSE: What happened to the traveller who brought the letter?

DAGOBERT: He went north, further into Siberia.

EVA: Thank you for your kindness.

JOSEPH: Do not thank me. Did not He say: 'Love one another'?

DAGOBERT: As soon as the traveller had left, misfortune fell upon us.

ROSE: Alas. Our mother.

DAGOBERT: Another traveller had arrived in the village. The cholera. When you returned from the forest with wild flowers for your mother, she was already in her last agony, hardly recognisable.

EVA: Here. My little Rose.

She hangs the medal round Rose's neck.

EVA: You must go to Paris. Dagobert will take you.

BLANCHE: We watched with her all night.

ROSE: In the morning we closed her eyes.

Scene 6

The stables.

Morok holds a long, heated iron bar.

MOROK: La Mort. La Mort. Look at me. La Mort, come here.

Scene 5a

ROSE: Dagobert, what does this medal mean? 'Victim of the Company. Pray for me.'

BLANCHE: And this date? 'Be at No 3 Rue St Francois, Paris, on the 13th February, 1832.'

DAGOBERT: It means, my children, that you must keep an appointment made for you a hundred and fifty years ago.

ROSE: With whom is this appointment?

DAGOBERT: I do not know. All I know is that you must be in Paris on the 13th of February.

Scene 6a

Wild neighing.

Ferocious roaring.

Scene 5b

DAGOBERT: Jovial. My horse.

A hand passes through the broken pane,

and smashes the lamp.

Complete darkness.

Scene 6b

La Mort's eyes are globes of phosphorescent light.

Her rounded ears cling to her skull, flat as a viper's head.

Jovial's neck is outstretched, his eye fixed. He is rigid with fear.

An icy sweat rolls down Jovial's flanks.

La Mort flings herself against the bars of her cage.

Jovial rushes at the closed door.

La Mort tries to force the iron bars.

Jovial strikes out violently with his forefeet.

Morok approaches the panther's cage. He slides back the heavy bolt.

La Mort throws herself at the bars. They yield.

Jovial rears.

La Mort fastens her teeth in his throat.

La Mort buries her sharp claws in his chest. Jovial's jugular vein opens. A torrent of bright red blood spouts forth.

DAGOBERT: I am here, Jovial. Help me, someone, help me open this door.

La Mort crushes Jovial to the ground, and buries her bloody face in the horse's entrails.

DAGOBERT: My horse. Jovial.

MOROK: Keep away. The panther is mad.

DAGOBERT: Save my horse. Help. One of his wild animals has escaped from its cage.

MOROK: La Mort. Come here. La Mort.

A ferocious roar –

A cry from Morok –

The panther howls plaintively.

MOROK: I thank thee, my God, that I have again been able to conquer, with the strength which Thou gavest me.

DAGOBERT: My old companion. Thou shalt answer to me for my horse's death.

MOROK: You tied your horse badly and he strayed into the shed. I shall be disabled for life. Look at my hand. Let go of me.

The burgomaster.

He will decide who is right or wrong.

DAGOBERT: Yes. That is fair. I must not take the law into my own hands.

The burgomaster.

Make way for the burgomaster.

A big man, of about sixty.

A cloth cap.

A cloak.

DAGOBERT: I am not responsible for this.

BURGOMASTER: Mr Morok disagrees. He is a pious and honest man, incapable of lying.

DAGOBERT: But surely you must hear my story?

BURGOMASTER: I have seen the frightful wound in the animal tamer's hand.

DAGOBERT: If he had kept the cage locked –

BURGOMASTER: You should have fastened your horse securely.

DAGOBERT: Someone untied my horse.

BURGOMASTER: Well, you are probably both to blame. You tethered your horse badly and the animal tamer left the door open. You need not pay him any damages.

DAGOBERT: And what does he owe me?

BURGOMASTER: You owe M. Morok nothing, and he owes you nothing.

DAGOBERT: I wish I were simply wounded in the hand. At least then I would be able to continue my journey.

BURGOMASTER: You are very concerned about your journey. You have papers, I presume?

DAGOBERT: Papers?

BURGOMASTER: Yes. You must have papers. Please show them to me.

Rose brings Dagobert's knapsack.

DAGOBERT: What is this?

BLANCHE: Is something wrong, Dagobert?

DAGOBERT: Gone. Everything gone.

ROSE: What dost thou seek?

BURGOMASTER: Lost your papers, eh?

DAGOBERT: I do not understand – my cross, money – papers. All gone. I beg you, for the sake of these orphans.

BURGOMASTER: Orphans.

MOROK: M. Burgomaster. I have something else to tell you about this man.

BURGOMASTER: What is that, Mr Morok?

MOROK: Look at him closely, M. Burgomaster. This man has a dangerous face.

DAGOBERT: If you have anything to say, say it out loud.

ROSE: Dagobert, be calm.

BURGOMASTER: You are a French spy. And these girls. Well, just look at them. Little innocents? Ladies of the night.

DAGOBERT: These are the daughters of a Marshal of France.

BURGOMASTER: Our Leipzig prisons will welcome a French agitator and a pair of female vagrants.

Dagobert rushes towards the Burgomaster.

He dashes him violently to the floor.

The Burgomaster is winded.

Dagobert catches Morok by his long hair.

Clasps his hand over his mouth.

Throws him to the ground.

Morok is dazed.

DAGOBERT: My children, we must flee before we are arrested and thrown in prison. Come.

MOROK: Unchain the dogs. Bring lanterns. Arm yourselves. They must not escape.

Scene 7

India.

Where flowers conceal dangerous reptiles.

Where bright fruits contain subtle poisons.

Pondicherry.

The end of October, 1831.

The sun spreads a sheet of dazzling light over the blue enamel sky.

Tall ferns.

Moist, humid.

Strong, sharp scents.

Cinnamon, ginger.

Jasmin.

An ajoupa, a tent made from cane mats suspended from tall bamboo poles.

Within the ajoupa a young man lies asleep.

A robe of white muslin. Tied with a scarlet sash.

Round his neck is a medal.

His blue-black hair, parted on his forehead, falls in waves.

Long eyelashes cast a shadow on his smooth cheek.

Bright red lips slightly apart.

Not a breath of air.

The tall ferns move.

A man.

His body is oiled and shining.

Long black hair bound about his temples.

He glides into the tent.

Djalma is restless with the heat.

Large drops of sweat lie like pearls on his skin.

The stranger draws a sharp needle from his belt.

He traces a mystical design on Djalma's arm.

Scene 8

Shelves filled with ledgers.

Cashbooks lying open on the desks.

The window protected by strong iron bars.

Joshua van Dael.

Merchant.

Educated in India at a school belonging to the Company of Jesus.

DAEL: To M. Rodin, Paris. I understand that Prince Djalma must be prevented from boarding ship for Europe. There is here a dangerous community whose members call themselves 'Brothers of the Good Work', or the 'Stranglers'. I have enlisted the aid of one such, Faringhea, offspring of a white father and an Indian mother. Like Prince Djalma, he too is fleeing from the English.

FARINGHEA: It is done.

Faringhea.

About 40 years old.

Poorly clad, in European fashion.

DAEL: So quickly.

FARINGHEA: Our brothers are swift and silent.

DAEL: Excellent.

FARINGHEA: And the money?

DAEL: Of course. A man must be rewarded for his work.

FARINGHEA: Well?

DAEL: I will pay you when the ship has sailed for Europe – with this letter on board – and without the Prince.

FARINGHEA: What of the Prince? Now he has our mark on him?

DAEL: I have done with him. You may have him for yourselves – for your gods.

FARINGHEA: We have only one goddess. Bohwanie.

DAEL: Ah yes.

FARINGHEA: Bohwanie watches over us.

DAEL: She has not helped you very much with the English.

FARINGHEA: We are strong with Bohwanie.

DAEL: You need money and armies, not goddesses. If the English have their way, you will either be killed or forced out of India.

FARINGHEA: The English may force us out of India, but behind us we leave our brethren, secret, numerous and terrible as the black scorpions. For us there is neither country nor family. Our brethren are our family, the world is our country.

DAEL: Noble words. Here is the letter.

FARINGHEA: And the money?

DAEL: Later.

Faringhea strangles van Dael.

Scene 7a

Djalma dreams of Paris.

He dreams of the city where his mother was born.

Where he can be safe from the English.

A city of gold.

FARINGHEA: Prince Djalma.

DJALMA: Who art thou?

FARINGHEA: A friend. Come to warn you. You are travelling across the sea?

DJALMA: How dost thou know?

FARINGHEA: I was told by the man who plans to stop you.

DJALMA: I do not believe thee.

FARINGHEA: Look at your arm.

DJALMA: The mark of the Stranglers. Who has done this?

FARINGHEA: The man who wishes to harm you.

DJALMA: I see.

FARINGHEA: The English killed your father and drove you from your province. You are planning to travel to Paris. I, too, am bound for that city. I have a letter to deliver. The French hate the English. They may help us. Perhaps we may travel together? I could serve you.

DJALMA: Thou art a friend. Come.

Scene 9

Paris.

No 11 Rue du Milieu-des-Ursins.

The end of October, 1831.

A simple house at the end of a dark, narrow courtyard.

On the ground floor, a large, quiet room.

At one end, a globe, four feet in diameter.

Dozens of small red crosses scattered all over the globe, from north to south, from east to west, from the most primitive countries to the centre of civilisation, to France itself.

Rodin is writing.

About fifty.

He wears a shabby coat, with a greasy collar.

A snuff-taker's cotton handkerchief for a cravat.

Trousers of threadbare black cloth.

Limp grey hair fringes his bald head.

Sharp black eyes.

Colourless thin lips.

A bell rings twice.

Doors open and shut.

The Abbé d'Aigrigny is tall and elegant.

His eyes are brilliant as polished steel.

He is forty-five years old.

A broad forehead, strong chest and shoulders.

His light chestnut hair is not yet silvered by time.

He wears a long frock coat.

Perfect gloves and boots. A light perfume hangs about him.

ABBE: Are there any letters from Dunkirk, M. Rodin?

RODIN: From Dunkirk?

ABBE: My mother is ill.

RODIN: Ah. I hope this will not delay your journey to Rome?

ABBE: No, no, of course not. Have you finished decoding the correspondence from abroad?

RODIN: Here it is.

ABBE: Read it to me.

RODIN: Father Orsini writes from Milan to thank us for the little book in which the French are represented as impious and debauched. It will be distributed throughout their schools.

ABBE: Excellent.

RODIN: Count Romanov of Riga writes that his father has died of the cholera. The epidemic is advancing slowly from the north of Russia, via Poland.

ABBE: May France be spared. Are you sure there is no news of my mother?

RODIN: Not as far as I know.

ABBE: Have you received the reports on the Rennepont affair?

RODIN: I have them.

ABBE: Read the reports.

RODIN: A hundred and fifty years ago a French Protestant family voluntarily exiled themselves, wishing to avoid the decrees issued against the enemies of our holy religion. Some of this family took refuge in the Indian colonies, some in Poland, some in Germany, some in England, some in America. Today there are six descendants left. The desmoiselles Rose and Blanche Simon. Prince Djalma. Jacques Rennepont, a workman. Mademoiselle Adrienne de Cardoville. The Abbé Gabriel Rennepont. Each member of this family possesses a bronze medal on which are engraved the following inscriptions: 'Victim of the Company, pray for me. Paris, 13th February, 1682. Be at No 3, Rue St Francois, Paris, on the 13th of February, 1832. Pray for me.' All six descendants are due to attend this family meeting appointed a century and a half ago.

ABBE: The Abbé Gabriel must be the only one present.

RODIN: There is a letter from Germany. From M. Morok.

ABBE: Read it.

RODIN: The daughters of Marshal Simon and the old man have arrived at the inn of the White Falcon, Leipzig. They will be relieved of their horse, money and papers, and detained as vagrants. They will not be in Paris by February 13th.

ABBE: Good.

RODIN: Joshua van Dael writes from Pondicherry that Prince Djalma is to be arrested as a suspected member of the notorious Indian Stranglers. He will be unable to reach France by February 13th.

ABBE: Very good.

RODIN: Jacques Rennepont, called Couche-tout-nu, lives in Paris. Drunken, idle, riotous. One of our agents has befriended his mistress, Cephyse Soliveau, also known as the Queen of the Revels. Our agent has seduced them into a life of riotous extravagance. Rennepont does not know of the meeting, and will certainly not be there on February 13th.

ABBE: Excellent.

RODIN: Mademoiselle Adrienne Rennepont de Cardoville. Lives in Paris. An extraordinary red-haired beauty. A remarkably original mind, an immense fortune, and all the sensual instincts one would expect in a girl of her age. Her rebelliousness makes her the most difficult to deal with. But even she will not be at the Rue St Francois on February 13th.

ABBE: And the Abbé Gabriel?

RODIN: The Abbé Gabriel Rennepont. He is an orphan adopted by Francoise Baudoin, the wife of Dagobert. She is a pious creature, guided in all things by her confessor. Gabriel has been in America, working as a missionary. His superiors in Charlestown are sending him back to Paris. When he arrives, we shall keep him confined until the 13th of February.

ABBE: Any other reports?

RODIN: No. That is all. Oh – well, well. I didn't notice this. It must have slipped between the other papers.

ABBE: My mother. Oh my God.

RODIN: What has happened?

ABBE: She has had a relapse. I must go to her at once.

RODIN: How unfortunate. You will not have time to visit her before you go to Rome.

ABBE: Not answer my mother's call? It would kill her.

RODIN: And your duty?

ABBE: My duty. Yes. You are right. File everything.

RODIN: I shall.

ABBE: Write to India, Germany and America. Put a close watch on Couche-tout-nu and Adrienne de Cardoville, and keep the Baudoin family under careful surveillance.

RODIN: Very well.

ABBE: I must hurry.

RODIN: Pondicherry, Leipzig, Charlestown. And Rome.

Scene 10

A man stands on a hillside.

Below, a wild, rugged valley.

A road leads through the villages.

It is the quiet hour, when every cottage normally brightens to the joyous blaze of the fire.

Now, every hearth is cold and deserted.

Every steeple rings out a funeral knell.

People appear in the dark villages

– advancing slowly towards the churchyards.

So many dead.

Hardly enough of the living left to bury them.

JOSEPH: I am Joseph, a shoemaker from Jerusalem. An artisan kept in misery, my misfortunes made me cruel. I bent over my work, sullen with hate and despair. The Saviour, carrying his cross, passed before my house. Sweat poured from him, his feet were bleeding. He asked if he could rest on a stone bench outside my house. I refused, crying 'I suffer and no-one helps me. Go on!' With a deep sigh of pain, the Saviour answered: 'Thou too shalt go on till the end of time.' And so my punishment began. Too late I understood the words 'Love one another.'

HERODIAS: I am Herodias, the wife of Herod's brother. When John the Baptist warned Herod against me, I was angered. When my daughter Salome danced before Herod, he offered her anything she wished. I instructed her to ask Herod for the head of John the Baptist.

JOSEPH: For my sin, I am condemned to wander till the day of Judgement.

HERODIAS: For my sin, I, too, am

condemned to wander till the day of Judgement.

JOSEPH: Joseph, the Wandering Jew.

HERODIAS: Herodias, the Wandering Jewess.

JOSEPH: Our hearts beat in unison. We wander the world.

HERODIAS: Meeting once a year, across the Bering Straits, at the time of the equinox.

JOSEPH: Here we follow the fortunes of a family through whom we may expiate our sins. On the thirteenth of February, six of my descendants are due to meet in Paris. At this moment I know that those I love are in great danger. But when I stretch out my hand to help – the whirlwind carries me away. Herodias. Help me.

HERODIAS: I cannot help you.

A stranger travels across the world –

– slow as eternity –

–implacable as fate.

This traveller is the cholera.

The cholera travels six leagues a day.

It advances slowly, at walking pace.

The cholera has passed through India.

The cholera has passed through Siberia.

The cholera is travelling towards France.

Scene 11

Paris.

February the 8th, 1832.

The Rue Brise Miche.

An alley, eight feet wide.

Enclosed by black, slimy walls.

No air, no light.

Fog.

A tall, narrow building.

Water oozes from the walls –

– and trickles down the filthy staircase.

The drains stink.

One room.

A single candle.

Grey paper covers the uneven wall.

A clean counterpane on the bed.

A small, iron stove with a large pot.

A plaster crucifix.

Images of saints, crudely coloured.

Francoise Baudoin, Dagobert's wife, lives here.

Francoise is preparing her son's evening meal.

From a small leather bag she takes an old silver cup and a spoon so worn and thin that it cuts like a knife.

Dagobert's wedding present. Her only silver. She puts a bottle of wine three-quarters full near her son's plate.

She is about fifty years old.

Years of hard work have ruined her sight.

Once an excellent needlewoman, now she can sew only coarse sacks for the army.

A young woman.

Eighteen years old.

Cruelly deformed.

Her pale face is marked by the smallpox.

Her magnificent brown hair is twisted into a large knot.

Magdalene Soliveau, nicknamed La Mayeux. Hunchback.

MAYEUX: I have brought some charcoal.

FRANCOISE: Thank you, my dear, Mayeux.

MAYEUX: Do you need any help?

FRANCOISE: No, thank you. The supper is ready.

La Mayeux and her sister Cephyse, were born in this house.

Orphaned when young, they were left in great poverty.

Cephyse was one of those vivacious restless natures who need air, movement and excitement.

Seduced by offers of food, warmth, fine clothes and freedom, Cephyse yielded to an attorney's clerk.

There were others and soon she was the idol of a world of students and clerks. She is known to everyone by the royal title of 'Queen of the Revels'.

La Mayeux makes shirts. Collars, cuffs, buttonholes, buttons, working without break twelve to fifteen hours a day. She makes fourteen to sixteen shirts a week. She earns four francs a week.

Half the pay of men working as tailors.

No fresh air.

Inadequate shelter.

No warm clothing.

No wholesome food.

Three kilos of inferior bread. Eighty-four centimes. Four pails of water.

Dripping or lard. Butter is too dear.

Grey salt.

A bushel of charcoal.

A litre of dried vegetables.

Three litres of potatoes.

Candles.

Needle and thread. All together, three francs nine centimes.

To save lighting the fire, she makes soup two or three times a week on a charcoal stove on the landing.

On the other days she eats the soup cold.

She has ninety-one centimes left for lodging, clothing and heating.

Agricola has an understanding with the porter, who lets her have a garret in the roof for twelve francs a year. Agricola pays the other eighteen francs, secretly.

A young man.

Twenty-four.

Tall, strong.

A smock stained by the smoke of the forge.

A cravat tied carelessly round his neck.

Cloth cap with a narrow peak.

He is holding a magnificent deep purple flower.

AGRICOLA: Good evening, dear Mother, And Mayeux.

FRANCOISE: Thou art late, Agricola. I've been worried.

AGRICOLA: Worried about me or my supper?

He kisses his mother.

FRANCOISE: Be careful. Wouldst thou make me spill the dinner?

AGRICOLA: Certainly not, dear Mother. It smells delicious. What is it?

FRANCOISE: Wait and see.

AGRICOLA: Mmm. Potatoes and bacon. I love potatoes and bacon.

FRANCOISE: On a Saturday?

AGRICOLA: Ah, true. On Saturday we are meant to fast. Well. Here are my wages.

FRANCOISE: Thanks, my child. And what a beautiful flower.

MAYEUX: In the middle of winter.

AGRICOLA: It smells of a mixture of vanilla and orange.

FRANCOISE: Where didst thou find it?

AGRICOLA: I have had an adventure. On my way home I found a little dog. It was wearing a collar. Mademoiselle Adrienne de Cardoville, Rue de Babylone, No 7. I picked up the dog, went to the house, rang the bell and a young lady opened the door.

GEORGETTE: Ah. You have found her. Mademoiselle Adrienne will be so pleased.

AGRICOLA: I saw gold and light and crystal and flowers. And in the middle of it all, a young lady of such heavenly beauty, with rich red hair, black eyes, rosy lips and a soft, white skin.

GEORGETTE: Mademoiselle. This young man has found Lutine.

ADRIENNE: Ah sir, I am indebted to you. Permit me –

AGRICOLA: And she holds out a purse.

MAYEUX: How she misunderstood thee.

AGRICOLA: She saw that I was hurt by the offer, so she takes this superb flower from a china vase.

ADRIENNE: At least you will accept this flower.

FRANCOISE: How well she understood my Agricola.

ADRIENNE: I am most grateful to you. If I can ever help you in any way, please do not hesitate to ask.

FRANCOISE: It is like a fairy tale. Is it not, Mayeux?

MAYEUX: Yes, Madame Francoise. Now, Agricola, wash thy hands before supper.

AGRICOLA: Thanks, Mayeux. Thou art kind. Here. Thou shalt have the flower for thyself.

MAYEUX: Thou wilt really give it to me? Thanks, Agricola.

FRANCOISE: Come, sit down and eat.

AGRICOLA: Wilt thou not eat with me, La Mayeux?

MAYEUX: I have dined.

AGRICOLA: Like my mother, who prefers to dine alone, that she may stint herself without my knowing it.

FRANCOISE: It suits my health better to dine early. Is it good?

AGRICOLA: Good? Excellent. Salt cod and turnips.

FRANCOISE: Next Friday and Saturday thou shalt have the same.

AGRICOLA: Not too much of a good thing, Mother.

FRANCOISE: If thy father could only see thee now.

AGRICOLA: He will see me soon enough.

FRANCOISE: Heaven grant thou mayst be right.

AGRICOLA: Heaven ought to grant it. Thou prayst enough.

FRANCOISE: Agricola.

AGRICOLA: Forgive me, Mother. In his last letter Father said he would be in Paris by the end of January.

FRANCOISE: Yes, child. And here we are in February.

AGRICOLA: Then we shall not have long to wait.

FRANCOISE: Alas, poor Baudoin, he must have suffered so. Separated from us, and now over sixty years of age. And he comes back to misery.

A knock on the door. Agricola goes to answer.

AGRICOLA: My good mother. Promise to be calm.

FRANCOISE: Thou alarmst me, Agricola.

AGRICOLA: Great joy can do as much harm as great grief.

FRANCOISE: Great joy?

AGRICOLA: Come, Mother, be brave.

FRANCOISE: After eighteen years. Oh, Agricola.

AGRICOLA: Mother –

FRANCOISE: Why art thou waiting? Let him in. Hurry.

Dagobert and the twins appear.

Francoise falls to her knees in prayer.

Agricola raises her.

Dagobert and Francoise embrace.

DAGOBERT: My children, this is my dear wife, Francoise. And these are the daughters of General Simon.

BLANCHE: Blanche and Rose.

DAGOBERT: And Agricola. Let me look at thee. What a well-grown, good looking fellow thou art.

FRANCOISE: Your hands are like ice. Oh, dear. The fire in the stove has gone out. Come, I will warm your hands in mine.

MAYEUX: I will fetch some more charcoal.

She takes the flower.

ROSE: You are not as we expected you, M. Agricola.

BLANCHE: Much more handsome.

FRANCOISE: These young ladies will want some supper.

DAGOBERT: Are you hungry, children?

ROSE: We are too happy to be hungry.

FRANCOISE: You will take a little hot wine with some water and sugar to warm you. I shall make the bed with clean white sheets. Dagobert, some supper for thee?

DAGOBERT: I will eat soon enough. For now, it is enough that my eyes feast on you all.

MAYEUX: Agricola, I must speak to thee.

DAGOBERT: Is something wrong?

MAYEUX: Alone.

AGRICOLA: It is nothing, Father. (*To* MAYEUX:) As soon as I can.

Scene 12

La Mayeux sits on her bed.

The purple flower perfumes the room.

AGRICOLA: Mayeux. My father is asleep.

MAYEUX: When I went to fetch the charcoal, I found this. Look.

AGRICOLA: 'Someone who is aware of the fraternal interest you feel for Agricola Baudoin, informs you that this honest worker will be arrested tomorrow.'

MAYEUX: Go on.

AGRICOLA: 'Several copies of his "Song of the Free Workers" have been found. They are clearly being used to foster insurrection against the government.' This is absurd. My songs celebrate the dignity of labour.

MAYEUX: A warrant has been issued against thee.

AGRICOLA: It's a joke. A hoax.

MAYEUX: What if it isn't?

AGRICOLA: The song was published two months ago. Why have they waited till now to prosecute?

MAYEUX: Thy verses deplore the misery of poor workers and pray for their deliverance.

AGRICOLA: They do not arrest a man for that.

MAYEUX: They arrest him first and hear him afterwards. In a month or two they may set him free.

AGRICOLA: A month without work. Without money. How will Mother live? And now Father is back. And the children.

MAYEUX: The young lady who gave thee the flower. Why not address thyself to her?

AGRICOLA: How can she help?

MAYEUX: Did she not tell thee to call on her if thou hadst need?

AGRICOLA: Yes.

MAYEUX: Ask her if she will stand bail for thee. The bail is nothing to her. To thee, a worker, it is everything. Thy family depends on it.

AGRICOLA: But what is the service I did her compared with what I have to ask?

MAYEUX: Dost thou think that a generous soul measures the services it renders by those it has received?

AGRICOLA: Not everyone is as generous as thou, Mayeux.

MAYEUX: Thou wilt at least ask her? Tomorrow?

AGRICOLA: Very well. I will go.

MAYEUX: I will watch the street for thee in the morning. Goodnight, Agricola.

Scene 12a

MAYEUX (*journal*): I love Agricola. No one will ever know. We have grown up as brother and sister, and no-one is surprised at my affection for him. I find some joy in being of use to him, if I can be nothing more.

Scene 13

Dagobert is shaved and dressed.

He holds Agricola's hands in his.

DAGOBERT: I shall savour thy face and thy voice every day. I am unused to such happiness. Come, let us plan our day. We shall take a walk together.

AGRICOLA: Father, I am afraid I cannot.

DAGOBERT: But today is Sunday.

AGRICOLA: I promised to go to the forge to finish some work.

DAGOBERT: Oh, dear. I had hoped – but how unjust I am. Grumbling about a walk delayed for a few hours, when for eighteen years I hardly knew whether I would see thee again.

Gabriel.

Long fair hair.

An angelic expression of goodness.

His eyes are clear, limpid.

His features are exquisite.

GABRIEL: Agricola?

AGRICOLA: My brother – Gabriel. Oh, Dagobert. Gabriel has arrived.

GABRIEL: M. Dagobert. I am so glad to meet thee.

DAGOBERT: My boy. It is good to see thee at last. What is that mark upon thy forehead?

GABRIEL: In the Rocky Mountains in America, those opposed to my teaching tortured me.

DAGOBERT: But thy comrades –

GABRIEL: I was alone.

AGRICOLA: Hadst no arms?

GABRIEL: We may not bear arms, brother. We cannot impart faith by force, only by persuasion.

AGRICOLA: And when persuasion fails?

GABRIEL: We die for our beliefs.

DAGOBERT: Then thy wounds are glorious.

GABRIEL: Pray, do not flatter me.

DAGOBERT: I do not flatter thee. When I charged the enemy, were not my companions with me? I had pride, battle cries, the smell of powder, the flourish of trumpets, to urge me on. I pass for a brave fellow. But thou art a thousand times braver.

GABRIEL: Do not exalt my courage over yours. You must be strong to behold the carnage of battle. We are protected from having to kill.

MAYEUX: Agricola – thou must make haste.

AGRICOLA: Mayeux – look – Gabriel is here.

MAYEUX: Agricola – the street is clear.

GABRIEL: I will not delay thee, Agricola. My visit must be short.

DAGOBERT: But Gabriel – thou hast come home.

GABRIEL: I have returned to Paris, but I am not free to return home.

DAGOBERT: Not free?

GABRIEL: My superior, Father Rodin, has ordered me to remain close to him.

DAGOBERT: But why? Is he sending thee on another mission?

GABRIEL: I do not know. M. Rodin has forbidden me to visit you after today.

DAGOBERT: Thy superior is a cruel man, Gabriel, if he separates thee from thy family.

GABRIEL: He is my superior, M. Dagobert.

AGRICOLA: Father, it is late. I must go.

DAGOBERT: Embrace me, then, and go.

GABRIEL: And I embrace thee, Agricola.

Scene 14

A winter sun rises in a clear blue sky.

The Hotel de St Dizier is one of the finest mansions in the Rue de Babylone.

Stern.

Gloomy.

Imposing.

At the end of the garden there is a pavilion shaped like a rotunda.

The glittering white stone is carved into wreaths, garlands, and fat little cupids.

Georgette.

Eighteen years old.

Bright eyes.

White teeth.

Pink ribbons.

A spring in her step.

Mme Augustine Grivois.

About fifty years old.

Dressed in black.

GRIVOIS: Mademoiselle. Mademoiselle Georgette.

GEORGETTE: Mme Grivois. To what am I indebted, Madame, for the pleasure of seeing you so early?

GRIVOIS: I must see Mademoiselle Adrienne immediately.

GEORGETTE: Mademoiselle went to bed very late. She has forbidden me to wake her before nine.

GRIVOIS: The Princess wishes to see her.

GEORGETTE: I know.

GRIVOIS: Then wake her immediately.

GEORGETTE: I shall wake her at the time she ordered and not a minute earlier.

GRIVOIS: I shall wake her myself.

GEORGETTE: Florine will not open the door.

GRIVOIS: You are an impertinent creature. Would you dare to disobey the Princess?

GEORGETTE: The Princess is not my mistress.

GRIVOIS: That, my girl, is where you are seriously mistaken. You will pay for your disrespect.

GEORGETTE: Oh yes. Whom shall I pay?

GRIVOIS: You and your mistress will both pay.

Scene 15

A temple, dedicated to beauty.

Mademoiselle de Cardoville has just left her bath.

She sits before her dressing table. Attended by her maids, Georgette and Florine.

Florine is tall and dark.

Statuesque as the Goddess Diana.

Adrienne de Cardoville's waist is as slender as that of a child of twelve.

Her swan-like neck is bare.

Droplets of water roll down the undulating line of her shoulders like beads of crystal on white marble.

A mass of red hair, luminous as molten gold.

Fine as silk —

So long –

She might wrap herself in it, like the Venus Aphrodite.

ADRIENNE: Florine, Georgette. Listen. An Indian Prince, twenty years old, a relation of mine, has arrived in Paris. Prince Djalma. He has come to fulfil an obligation in his mother's will. He is destitute, having been forced to leave India. His loyal servant, M. Faringhea, writes to me secretly, so that his master should not be embarrassed by asking for help. Such nobility of conscience. He suggests a small sum of money to purchase clothes. Just imagine. A handsome young prince from the land of the East where men are dressed in silk and muslin and cashmere. A brave, good, young, handsome man, without any resources. I shall help him. Florine.

FLORINE: I await your commands, Mademoiselle.

ADRIENNE: I shall send him some money that his servant may settle them comfortably in a house in the Rue Blanche. When he is at ease here, then I shall cast my eye upon this Indian Bacchus. You will deliver the letter for me.

FLORINE: Certainly, Mademoiselle.

GEORGETTE: Mademoiselle, the workman who came yesterday begs to speak with you a moment.

AGRICOLA: Mademoiselle – excuse this interruption.

ADRIENNE: M. Baudoin.

AGRICOLA: Mademoiselle. Yesterday you offered me your purse. I refused it. Today, I have come to ask for ten, perhaps twenty times the amount.

ADRIENNE: You are in difficulty?

AGRICOLA: Mademoiselle, my family depends upon my labour and if I am put out of work, my mother will be without resources.

ADRIENNE: I will see that your mother will want for nothing.

AGRICOLA: You are generous.

ADRIENNE: It is easy to be generous when one has wealth.

AGRICOLA: My father has just returned home after many years in exile, with two orphans, daughters of his commander, Marshal Simon.

ADRIENNE: Marshal Simon? Why, he is a distant relation of mine.

AGRICOLA: Then the children – oh, Mademoiselle, what will become of them all if I am arrested?

ADRIENNE: Arrested? But what have you done?

AGRICOLA: I write poems, simple songs. In these troubled times, it seems even that is considered dangerous. I have been warned that I am to be arrested.

ADRIENNE: You would like me to stand bail?

AGRICOLA: Mademoiselle.

ADRIENNE: I have already said I would help you. And the daughters of Marshal Simon are part of my family.

GEORGETTE: Mademoiselle, someone is asking for Agricola Baudoin.

AGRICOLA: I do not want to cause you trouble, Mademoiselle. Let me give myself up.

ADRIENNE: Liberty is too precious. You must stay here. You will be quite safe. You may even write some verses for me if you are so inspired.

Scene 16

GRIVOIS: Well?

FLORINE: Here are my notes.

GRIVOIS: Excellent. Any letters?

FLORINE: Yes, one.

GRIVOIS: Well?

FLORINE: I – sent it.

GRIVOIS: Sent it? Mademoiselle, you know that your orders are to tell me everything.

FLORINE: Madame – I am uneasy –

GRIVOIS: If you have scruples, you are at liberty to go.

FLORINE: You know very well that I am not at liberty, Madame. I am dependent on M. Rodin. But Mademoiselle is so good, so confiding.

GRIVOIS: She is all perfection, no doubt. But you are not here to sing her praises.

You are here to obey orders. Is there anything else?

FLORINE: The man who brought Lutine home yesterday is here again.

GRIVOIS: What does he want?

FLORINE: I do not know, Madame. I left to deliver these just as he arrived.

GRIVOIS: Well. Go back to the pavilion, and let me advise you to guard against any fine scruples.

FLORINE: I cannot forget, Madame, that I no longer have a will of my own.

Scene 17

The Princess de St Dizier waits in her grand salon.

She is still handsome at forty-five.

During the final years of the empire, she was one of the most beautiful and fashionable women in Paris.

She conducted a clandestine correspondence with a number of influential people well-known for their hatred of France and of Napoleon.

One of these was the Marquis d'Aigrigny.

Then a Colonel in the service of Russia.

When the conspiracy was uncovered, she was banished from Paris.

But at the Restoration, with the Abbé now serving under the new government, Madame again acquired considerable influence.

A closer liaison ensued between them.

After the duel, in which he was defeated by Marshal Simon, the Marquis unexpectedly entered a seminary and took Holy Orders.

The Princess followed his example and was converted.

She renounced all worldly vanities. Even her servants are dressed in black.

The Abbé is still her spiritual advisor.

GRIVOIS: Here are Florine's notes, Madame.

PRINCESS: Thank you. M. L'Abbé, you are in mourning?

ABBE: My mother.

PRINCESS: I am so sorry. Did you see her before she died?

ABBE: No, I was forced to sacrifice her to my duty. I am afraid I have never quite been able to attain that complete self-denial which is laid down in our constitution.

PRINCESS: 'If any man hate not his father and mother and his own life also, he cannot be my disciple.' But what power you have in return for this small sacrifice.

ABBE: True. I am a thousand times more powerful leading my black, silent militia, than ever I was commanding a regiment of soldiers.

PRINCESS: Exactly. You must not regret what is past. Look at me. Had it not been for you, I would still be surrounded by stupid men, who only want women to minister to their baser passions. Now I have men of influence near me who think only of our glorious future.

ABBE: There are some who are blind enough to believe that the Company of Jesus has no future. But after the 13th of February, they will all be proved wrong.

PRINCESS: What news is there of the medals?

ABBE: Rodin has told me of the arrival of General Simon's daughters. However, Mme Baudoin's confessor has his instructions. And plans are underway for that drunkard, Couche- tout-nu. All our hopes rest on Gabriel. M. Rodin is keeping him under constant watch, well away from his family. On my way back from Rome I stayed with the Duke d'Orbano. He wants five million francs, in return for which, we are to have sole charge of all the schools in his province.

PRINCESS: Five million francs.

ABBE: A small advance against our expectations.

Doctor Baleinier is fifty years old, plump, with a round shining face.

He wears black silk breeches.

One sleek white hand concealed beneath a cambric ruffle.

He takes communion once a week very publicly, at High Mass, in the Church of St Thomas Aquinas.

DOCTOR: I kiss your hand, Princess.

PRINCESS: Always so gallant, my dear M. Baleinier.

DOCTOR: M. l'Abbé.

PRINCESS: Does she suspect anything?

DOCTOR: Nothing. We are the best of friends. Only the other day I made some light-hearted observations on her eccentric mode of life, and she was highly amused. She really is a most remarkable young lady.

PRINCESS: Doctor, doctor, no weakness now.

DOCTOR: Weakness, Madame. Did I not propose the scheme to you myself?

ADRIENNE: You sent for me, Aunt?

PRINCESS: Yes, Mademoiselle. I wish to talk to you about a matter of the gravest importance.

ADRIENNE: Then we had better talk alone.

PRINCESS: We can talk freely here. These gentlemen are old family friends.

ADRIENNE: I do not doubt M. d'Aigrigny's friendship. And Dr Baleinier is one of my oldest friends. But I would still like to know what you wish to discuss before I can agree to their presence.

PRINCESS: I thought, Mademoiselle, that you pretended to value frankness.

ADRIENNE: Really, Aunt. I have no more pretension to frankness than you have to sincerity.

PRINCESS: I wish to inform you of my decisions for your future in the presence of family friends.

ADRIENNE: Your decisions?

PRINCESS: You do not respect me enough.

ADRIENNE: I assure you, Aunt, that I have never given the matter any thought.

PRINCESS: Well. I take the blame for that. I should have exerted my authority more forcefully. You are self-willed and headstrong. You must change.

ADRIENNE: I expect I may well change. One hears of such odd conversions.

ABBE: A sincere conversion can never be called odd, Mademoiselle.

ADRIENNE: That depends. For instance, if one converts defects into vices –

PRINCESS: What do you mean, Mademoiselle?

ADRIENNE: I am speaking of myself, Aunt. You reproach me with being self-willed and headstrong. Suppose I were to become hypocritical and wicked? I think I prefer to keep such minor faults as I already have. I know what I am. I do not know what I might become. But I do not think you have invited me here to discuss philosophy. What, Aunt, is the real object of this meeting?

PRINCESS: You are to submit to my orders with the obedience and respect which is due to me. Or else.

ADRIENNE: This is a declaration of war.

ABBE: We are not talking of declarations of war.

ADRIENNE: M. l'Abbé, as a former colonel you should be able to see the joke.

PRINCESS: Mademoiselle, your behaviour is intolerable.

ADRIENNE: What plan of conduct have you mapped out for me, Aunt?

PRINCESS: Mademoiselle. Six months ago at the end of the period of mourning for your father, you, being eighteen years old, asked me to relinquish control of your fortune. Unfortunately, I was weak enough to consent. You established yourself in the garden pavilion.

ADRIENNE: Correct.

PRINCESS: Since then you have not fulfilled any of your religious duties. You do not go to church. You go out alone without giving any account of your actions to anyone.

ADRIENNE: I live openly. I have nothing to hide.

PRINCESS: You have no conception of the meaning of duty or obedience.

ADRIENNE: And I will have none until duty and obedience come to me in a form that I can respect.

PRINCESS: From now on you will do nothing without my permission.

Adrienne laughs.

ABBE: Really, Mademoiselle.

ADRIENNE: How can I be serious when I hear my aunt talking of submission to her orders? Could a swallow used to sunshine agree to live with a mole in darkness?

DOCTOR: My dear Madame, Adrienne has a naturally excitable nature. She is the most charming mad woman I know. I have told her so a hundred times.

ABBE: Your attachment to Mademoiselle should not blind you to the extravagance of her words.

PRINCESS: Mademoiselle does not seem to comprehend the serious nature of this conference.

ADRIENNE: Let me hear your orders, then, Aunt.

PRINCESS: From tomorrow you will leave the pavilion. You will discharge your entirely unsuitable maids. You will occupy rooms in this house. You will never go out alone. You will accompany me to church. I will take charge of all your expenses, and ensure that you are modestly dressed.

ADRIENNE: I moved to the pavilion because I could no longer tolerate the hypocrisy in this house. I choose to spend my income myself, according to my own tastes. I do not go to Mass and if my mother were alive, she would understand and embrace me tenderly. I adore God in all the beauty He has made, fair and good and noble. If Doctor Baleinier has often found me prey to a strange excitement, it is because when the present is odious and painful, I imagine the future. Visions wrap me in a sublime ecstasy. I cherish sacred hopes that we might all, one day, have the power to choose our destinies.

DOCTOR: When will she be as reasonable as she is charming?

ADRIENNE: This very instant, my good Doctor. I have heard your plans. Now hear mine. I have decided to move to another house where I shall live in my own way.

PRINCESS: It is immoral for a young woman to live alone.

ADRIENNE: So many poor girls, orphans like myself, live alone and free, and yet they live honestly.

ABBE: There is no comparison, Mademoiselle, between people of the class you name and a young person of your rank.

ADRIENNE: For a Catholic, M. l'Abbé, that distinction is not very Christian.

ABBE: One day your family may wish you to marry.

ADRIENNE: If I marry, I will choose for myself.

PRINCESS: It is indecent, Mademoiselle, to speak thus.

ADRIENNE: I beg your pardon if I have shocked you. Now. This house belongs to me. I wish to offer hospitality to a young Indian prince, a distant relative.

ABBE: An Indian prince?

ADRIENNE: His name is Prince Djalma. And I have learned this morning that two of my relations on my mother's side, the daughters of Marshal Simon, are also in Paris.

PRINCESS: Is there anyone else you wish to add to this interesting family group?

GRIVOIS: Excuse me, Madame –

She whispers.

PRINCESS: Indeed. Will you accompany me, M. d'Aigrigny? Excuse me, Mademoiselle, Doctor.

The Abbé and the Princess leave.

ADRIENNE: Thank you for your courage in supporting me, Doctor.

DOCTOR: Pray do not say such things. You will get me into trouble with the Princess.

ADRIENNE: Do not be afraid. Doctor, I may need your help.

DOCTOR: In what way?

ADRIENNE: I believe you are closely acquainted with the Chief of Police.

DOCTOR: Yes. I am treating him for laryngitis.

ADRIENNE: I have a young protégé, on whose behalf I may need help. He is an honest workman –

PRINCESS: I have some news, Mademoiselle, which may interest you.

ADRIENNE: Excuse me, Madame.

PRINCESS: Where are you going?

ADRIENNE: You have expressed your will and I have told you mine. Good day to you.

The Princess seizes her arm.

PRINCESS: You do not want to hear my news, Mademoiselle? Are you afraid of something?

ADRIENNE: If there is anything stronger than the disgust you inspire in me, it is the fear of being accused of cowardice. Go on, Madame.

PRINCESS: Earlier this morning a ruffian wanted by the police was seen entering her house. The police have just searched the pavilion. This girl has deceived us.

ADRIENNE: What do you mean, Madame?

PRINCESS: In Mademoiselle's bedroom. No. It is too disgusting.

ADRIENNE: I have nothing to be ashamed of, Madame.

PRINCESS: A man concealed in her bedroom

DOCTOR: No doubt a thief.

PRINCESS: Your indulgence for Mademoiselle deceives you, M. Baleinier. I am no longer astonished by the sympathy Mademoiselle has professed for the lower orders. The man in her room is a labourer. A very handsome labourer.

ADRIENNE: Enough, Madame, enough. I will not defend myself against your odious insinuations.

PRINCESS: The man has been arrested. Does that not pierce your heart, Mademoiselle?

ADRIENNE: Dr Baleinier, I asked you just now about your influence with the Chief of Police.

DOCTOR: Mademoiselle, it will give me great pleasure to act on your behalf.

ADRIENNE: Your carriage is below?

DOCTOR: Yes, Mademoiselle.

ADRIENNE: You will be good enough to accompany me immediately to his house.

The Abbé looks at the Doctor.

The Doctor nods.

PRINCESS: Mademoiselle, I forbid you to leave.

ABBE: I think, Madame, we may entrust Mademoiselle to the Doctor's care.

PRINCESS: Very well.

ADRIENNE: Come, my dear Doctor.

Scene 18

DOCTOR: Wait in here. I will go and find the Chief of Police.

An iron grating covers the fireplace.

The tongs and shovel are fastened with iron chains.

The armchair is fastened to the floor.

A dull, heavy thud like that of a falling body.

Muffled moaning.

The door is locked.

Howling from the room above.

Stamping feet.

The window is barred.

In a lighted window opposite, a gaunt figure.

Wrapped in a jacket – unable to move.

ADRIENNE: Where am I?

A long dark night.

Scene 19

Night.

Dark and gloomy.

Sleet.

FRANCOISE: Children, come. Pray with me.

ROSE: We do not know any real prayers.

BLANCHE: We only pray to our mother, who is in heaven.

FRANCOISE: But what of your catechism, confirmation, communion?

BLANCHE: What are they, Madame?

FRANCOISE: Your souls are in the greatest peril, children.

MAYEUX: May I come in, Madame Francoise?

FRANCOISE: Of course.

MAYEUX: You must have courage, Madame.

FRANCOISE: La Mayeux, please tell me.

MAYEUX: This morning Agricola went to ask Mademoiselle de Cardoville for help. I have just come from her house. Florine, her maid, told me that Agricola has been arrested.

FRANCOISE: My son, arrested. Oh God.

MAYEUX: Thank God, M. Dagobert is here.

FRANCOISE: The Lord has visited this upon me.

MAYEUX: Madame Francoise –

FRANCOISE: Almighty Father, have I not suffered enough? Forgive me. If it is Thy will, I accept all Thou sendest me.

MAYEUX: We must tell Monsieur Dagobert.

FRANCOISE: No. He is asleep. He does not know that Agricola has not come home.

MAYEUX: But he will know what to do.

FRANCOISE: This is my sin, and I will expiate it. My good Mayeux. Take my silver cup, spoon and sheets to the pawnbrokers. Before Dagobert wakes.

Scene 20

A gloomy church.

Francoise enters the confessional.

A priest.

Rodin watches.

PRIEST: Speak, my daughter.

FRANCOISE: Last night I learned that my poor son had been arrested. Instead of submitting to this trial which the Lord had sent me, I rebelled against it.

PRIEST: Go on.

FRANCOISE: Alas, Father, I fear that I am on a path to still graver sins.

PRIEST: Speak.

FRANCOISE: My husband brought two young orphans with him. Father, they have not been baptised.

PRIEST: Then they are heathens.

FRANCOISE: If they should happen to commit a mortal sin, Father, I and my husband would be in mortal sin, since we are their guardians.

PRIEST: Does your husband observe his religious duties?

FRANCOISE: Grace has not yet touched his heart.

PRIEST: God is punishing you for your husband and son's lack of faith. But He is merciful, so long as you do not make the same mistake with the orphans. You must send these girls to a convent where they may be properly instructed.

FRANCOISE: We are too poor, Father.

PRIEST: I know the superior of a good and generous convent. They will bear all the costs.

FRANCOISE: I shall speak to my husband.

PRIEST: It must be done without his knowledge.

FRANCOISE: But Father, he is their guardian.

PRIEST: Can you instruct the children at home?

FRANCOISE: I cannot.

PRIEST: Are they exposed to impiety by remaining with you?

FRANCOISE: They are.

PRIEST: Then you have no choice.

FRANCOISE: What shall I say to my husband?

PRIEST: You will tell him that you cannot answer any questions about the girls.

FRANCOISE: I will do my duty as a Christian.

PRIEST: The Lord will reward you, daughter. I shall send a friend to collect the girls. Be sure that your husband is away from home this afternoon.

Scene 21

La Mayeux hurries with a heavy bundle.

A silver spoon falls to the ground.

POLICEMAN: Stop there, young woman. Did you hear me? Where did you get this silver?

MAYEUX: I – I – this, sir, is not mine. I am taking it to the pawnbroker's for a friend.

What's she got in her hump?

Boots.

Umbrellas.

Clocks.

Let's have a look. It's free, isn't it?

Don't shove.

Give us a kiss.

Let's have a proper look.

POLICEMAN: What else have you got there?

MAYEUX: Let me go –

POLICEMAN: Come on, let's have a look. Sheets, spoon, fork, a silver cup. Not bad. Dressed like a beggar, carrying silver. You've stolen more than your own weight.

MAYEUX: Stolen? No, sir.

Thief.

Arrest her.

POLICEMAN: Come on, you.

MAYEUX: Sir, let me explain.

POLICEMAN: You can explain later.

Scene 22

GRIVOIS: Your relative, Mademoiselle de Cardoville wishes so much to see you. And she has sent me to fetch you.

BLANCHE: May we go, Madame?

GRIVOIS: They will be back within the hour.

FRANCOISE: If this lady is kind enough to take you.

GRIVOIS: Well, then, young ladies.

BLANCHE: We shall not be long, Mme Francoise.

GRIVOIS: I look forward to seeing your relative's joy when she sees how alike you are.

ROSE: It would be strange if we were not alike. We have never been apart.

GRIVOIS: Really?

BLANCHE: Never, Madame.

GRIVOIS: Then how unhappy you would be if you were separated.

ROSE: Who would have the heart to separate us?

BLANCHE: It would cause us too much grief.

ROSE: It would kill us.

Scene 23

DAGOBERT: I have been walking for hours. Agricola did not go to the forge yesterday.

FRANCOISE: I am sure he will come back soon.

DAGOBERT: Where are the children?

FRANCOISE: They have gone out.

DAGOBERT: Gone out? Where have they gone?

FRANCOISE: You are like an old hen with her chickens.

DAGOBERT: Their dying mother entrusted them to my care.

FRANCOISE: Thou art right to love them.

DAGOBERT: Thou hast let them go out alone? When will they be back?

FRANCOISE: I do not know.

DAGOBERT: Thou dost not know? These children must have been very anxious to go out. Answer me.

FRANCOISE: Do with me what thou wilt, but do not ask me what has become of the children.

DAGOBERT: How canst thou expect me not to ask? Francoise. What is happening?

FRANCOISE: Mercy, mercy. Thou art hurting me.

DAGOBERT: Where are the children?

FRANCOISE: Alas, my dear.

DAGOBERT: It is no use crying 'alas'. What if the Marshal were to arrive? What would I say?

FRANCOISE: Blame me.

DAGOBERT: That will not bring the girls back. Are they well, at least?

FRANCOISE: Thank God, they are well.

DAGOBERT: Francoise – I have a duty to ensure that these children are in the Rue St Francois on the 13th of February.

FRANCOISE: The 13th February? Like Gabriel.

DAGOBERT: What has this to do with Gabriel?

FRANCOISE: When I took him in, he wore a bronze medal round his neck with that same place and date on it. I showed it to my confessor, and when Gabriel went to the Jesuit school, he gave it to M. Rodin, the gentleman who so kindly undertook his education.

DAGOBERT: A priest?

FRANCOISE: Why, yes.

DAGOBERT: Priests. Thy confessor may control thy life. He shall not control mine.

POLICEMAN: Mme Francoise Baudoin?

FRANCOISE: Yes, sir.

POLICEMAN: This young person says you know her.

FRANCOISE: Of course I do. Is something wrong, La Mayeux?

MAYEUX: You see, sir, that I am not a thief.

POLICEMAN: The silver cup, the shawl, the sheets in this bundle –

FRANCOISE: They are mine.

POLICEMAN: Then I have made a mistake, my dear.

MAYEUX: Thank you, sir.

DAGOBERT: Excuse me – I wish to report the abduction of two young girls. They were in my wife's care.

FRANCOISE: Do not say a word more, I entreat thee.

DAGOBERT: I accuse my wife's confessor of being responsible for the abduction of Marshal Simon's daughters. This morning I went out and I left the girls with my wife. When I returned they were gone.

POLICEMAN: Madame?

FRANCOISE: That is true, sir.

POLICEMAN: And where are the girls?

FRANCOISE: I cannot say.

DAGOBERT: Her confessor knows where they are.

POLICEMAN: Madame –

FRANCOISE: I cannot say any more, sir.

POLICEMAN: If you refuse to explain, I shall have to take you into custody.

DAGOBERT: Take her into custody?

MAYEUX: You cannot.

POLICEMAN: You have brought a serious charge, sir. According to your wife's own admission, she alone is compromised. The girls were in her care.

DAGOBERT: My wife will not leave this room.

FRANCOISE: My dear, the Lord is pleased to try me. I am his unworthy servant and must gratefully resign myself to His will.

DAGOBERT: She is mad.

MAYEUX: She cannot be arrested as well.

DAGOBERT: What do you mean?

MAYEUX: Agricola has been arrested.

FRANCOISE: Oh, Mayeux.

DAGOBERT: My son, arrested?

POLICEMAN: Come, Madame.

Scene 24

Dancers.

Singing as they cross the square.

Drunk.

Early morning workers.

Students.

Shop girls.

Clerks.

Mayeux has risen at daybreak.

The carnival breakfast is ordered for seven.

Where are they? Where's the carriage?

Where is the Queen of the Revels?

What a costume.

Dazzling.

Fantastic.

Have you seen her dance?

The full-blown tulip.

Bounding, weaving, twisting.

Have you seen Rennepont?

Drinks like a fish.

They've been together for three months.

She adores him.

He adores her.

He's paid for everything.

Coaches, breakfast at ten francs a head, musicians.

Make way for the Queen of the Revels.

Long live the Queen of the Revels.

Jacques Rennepont, Couche-tout-nu.

Twenty-five years old.

Scarlet waistcoat.

Trousers with broad blue stripes.

A hat covered with flowers and ribbons.

Rose Pompon. Seventeen.

Bright black eyes.

Red hair.

Tinsel!

Spangles!

Cephyse.

Queen of the Revels.

Twenty years old.

Magnificent chestnut hair.

Large blue eyes.

CEPHYSE: La Mayeux.

MAYEUX: Cephyse.

CEPHYSE: Come, join us.

MAYEUX: I cannot.

CEPHYSE: Then I shall join you.

They embrace.

CEPHYSE: Let me kiss you. Oh, my dear, It has been such a long time.

MAYEUX: You look wonderful, Cephyse.

CEPHYSE: I have never seen thee look so worn.

MAYEUX: I have been working late.

CEPHYSE: Oh, forgive us, Mayeux.

MAYEUX: My dear Cephyse, why dost thou ask my pardon?

CEPHYSE: Is it not shameful of me to be dressed in all this finery, whilst thou art so miserably clad?

MAYEUX: There is nothing shameful about it.

CEPHYSE: Thou canst console me in the midst of thine own misfortunes. Look. Jacques has some money left. Let me help thee.

MAYEUX: Thanks, my dear Cephyse. I do not need anything.

CEPHYSE: Thou canst not accept assistance from my lover.

MAYEUX: Cephyse, I did not mean to hurt thee.

CEPHYSE: I could never give up this way of life. It is precarious, but at least it is free. When we have money, we spend it.

MAYEUX: But my dear Cephyse, why not invest the money and marry Jacques?

CEPHYSE: Investing money is so boring. I like Jacques better than anyone, but if we were married all our happiness would end. As long as he is my lover, he cannot reproach me with my past.

MAYEUX: What will you do when the money has gone?

CEPHYSE: When the money runs out, there's always the charcoal fumes.

The Queen of the Revels.

We want the Queen of the Revels.

CEPHYSE: My court is growing impatient. Jacques, come here.

COUCHE: Long live the Queen of the Revels.

CEPHYSE: Jacques, this is my sister, La Mayeux.

COUCHE: Delighted to meet you, Mademoiselle.

CEPHYSE: My sister works as a seamstress.

MAYEUX: Alas, work is hard to come by now, Cephyse.

CEPHYSE: Jacques. We must help her.

COUCHE: Here, Mademoiselle, take this.

CEPHYSE: You are a true gentleman, Jacques. His father was only a rag and bone man. But he left him a small fortune.

COUCHE: Correction my darling. He left me a pile of old papers.

CEPHYSE: Ah yes. But who raised ten thousand francs on the strength of those old papers?

COUCHE: And who introduced me to the money-lender who was silly enough to advance money on them? My clever Cephyse.

MAYEUX: Thank you both.

CEPHYSE: Jacques, kiss me.

COUCHE: I shall kiss you now, and later, and then again and again and again.

MAYEUX: Monsieur Jacques, you are very generous. I will use the money as bail for a friend.

CEPHYSE: It could not be put to better use.

COUCHE: There is no need to thank me, Mademoiselle. Money is made to be shared.

We want the Queen of the Revels.

COUCHE: Excuse us, Mademoiselle. Royalty has its duties.

MAYEUX: When shall I see thee again?

CEPHYSE: Very soon. I promise.

Mayeux leaves.

CEPHYSE: They say that the cholera is approaching with his seven-league boots. A toast to the cholera.

COUCHE: My brave Cephyse.

CEPHYSE: To the cholera. Let him spare

those who wish to live and kill those who dread parting from one another.

ROSE POMPON: To the cholera. Let only the good be left alive.

CEPHYSE: And a toast to my darling Couche-tout-nu.

A quadrille!

The full-blown tulip!

They dance.

Waiter whispers.

COUCHE: I'll come directly. Someone take my place.

He goes.

CEPHYSE: What is it?

Waiter whispers.

COUCHE: He says I am to be arrested for debt.

CEPHYSE: For what debt?

COUCHE: The papers. The bill of exchange. The money lender now wants to call in the debt. Bastard.

CEPHYSE: There must be some mistake.

COUCHE: A money lender doesn't make mistakes. Where will I find ten thousand francs? And what will become of thee? At least I shall be fed in prison. How wilt thou live?

CEPHYSE: I will sell my clothes.

COUCHE: And then?

CEPHYSE: I will find work, and go and live with my sister. We've had a good time, haven't we?

COUCHE: Oh, Cephyse.

CEPHYSE: I shall wait for thee. I would rather die than take another lover.

COUCHE: My dear.

CEPHYSE: I do not care whether I live or die, as long as we are together.

COUCHE: Come, dry your eyes. Kiss me.

Scene 25

The pavilion in the Rue de Babylone.

FLORINE: La Mayeux. Will you take a little orange flower water and sugar?

MAYEUX: Thank you, Mademoiselle Florine.

FLORINE: Draw near the fire. How wet your feet are. Please. Rest them on this stool.

MAYEUX: You are obliging, Mademoiselle.

FLORINE: I wish I could help you more.

MAYEUX: You can help me. Would you beg your mistress to give me a few moments of her time? I need money for bail, for my adopted brother.

FLORINE: I am afraid Mademoiselle is not here.

MAYEUX: May I wait for her?

FLORINE: She is ill. Deranged. No one may see her.

MAYEUX: Deranged?

FLORINE: She became ill very suddenly and was taken away.

MAYEUX: Do you know where she is?

FLORINE: No. I am so worried. Look. While I was setting my mistress's room to rights, I found these: an envelope and a medal. I doubt she knows of their existence.

MAYEUX: Why, this is like the medal worn by the daughters of Marshal Simon.

FLORINE: I am sure it is important. It must not fall into the hands of my mistress's family. I cannot tell you more. Would you take the medal and keep it for my mistress until she returns? It is not safe here.

MAYEUX: But surely –

FLORINE: Please. I can trust you.

MAYEUX: Well –

FLORINE: Thank you. And – take this money. Perhaps it will help towards the bail.

MAYEUX: You are so kind, Mademoiselle. You look unhappy.

FLORINE: I would gladly change places with you.

MAYEUX: Surely not. I hope you may never know what it is to want work.

FLORINE: Are you in need of employment?

MAYEUX: Desperately. My employer has found someone to replace me for less than four francs a week.

FLORINE: Four francs! I think I can find you work which pays more than that.

MAYEUX: Is that possible?

FLORINE: Come. I will take you to see the Mother Superior.

Scene 26

Mother St Perpetue is about forty.

A white cap tied beneath her chin.

A long black veil round her thin, pale face.

Piercing black eyes.

The management of all the vast transactions of this community are mere child's play to Mother St Perpetue.

The price of stocks.

The rate of exchange.

The current value of shares.

She has never made a bad investment.

All for the benefit of the community.

PRINCESS: And how are the twins?

MOTHER: Placed in separate rooms, as you ordered. The separation has produced a fever, and great depression in both of them. It is remarkable. Their symptoms are identical.

PRINCESS: Are they well guarded?

MOTHER: The porters are all armed.

PRINCESS: Double your precautions. Their guardian has discovered their absence.

MOTHER: It will be done.

Scene 27

La Mayeux waits.

She sees a girl at one of the windows.

Red hair.

Mademoiselle de Cardoville.

MAYEUX: She cannot be mad.

Scene 28

MOTHER: My dear daughter. How may I help you?

MAYEUX: Florine has told me that you might know of some work for me. I am a seamstress.

MOTHER: Are you entirely unemployed?

MAYEUX: Alas, yes, Madame.

MOTHER: Call me Mother, my dear daughter.

MAYEUX: I have always lived honestly by my labour, Mother.

MOTHER: We must thank the Lord He has delivered you from temptation. Are you clever at your trade?

MAYEUX: I have always satisfied my employers.

MOTHER: We have about a hundred companions to ladies, young women in shops, servants and needlewomen, in a great number of families. You will understand that we only employ women of the greatest propriety.

MAYEUX: I understand, Mother.

MOTHER: It is our duty to give to masters and mistresses every possible reassurance as to the morality of the person that we place with them. Likewise we give the employee every reassurance as to the morality of their employers.

MAYEUX: Nothing could be more just, Mother.

MOTHER: A worker such as yourself is placed with persons whom we suppose irreproachable. Should she, however, perceive on the part of her employers or of the persons who frequent the house, any irregularity, she should immediately inform us.

MAYEUX: I could never inform on my employer.

MOTHER: You are honest. Let me embrace you. Now, tell me. How many times a month do you approach the Lord's table?

MAYEUX: Madame, I have not taken the sacrament since my first communion eight years ago.

MOTHER: And why is that, my dear?

MAYEUX: I have no time.

MOTHER: You are indeed honest. Thank you for coming to see me.

MAYEUX: You cannot employ me?

MOTHER: Not until you can find it in your heart to devote yourself to God.

MAYEUX: Madame, I beg your pardon for having detained you for so long.

Scene 29

La Mayeux looks up towards the window.

Adrienne comes out. Blanche approaches her.

The orphan speaks a few words to Adrienne.

A nun seizes Blanche roughly by the arm.

Mademoiselle de Cardoville appeals to her.

The nun drags the orphan away.

MAYEUX: Mademoiselle de Cardoville?

ADRIENNE: How do you know me?

MAYEUX: I am Agricola Baudoin's adopted sister.

ADRIENNE: Is he in prison?

MAYEUX: Yes. But I have found bail for him, and he is to be released today.

ADRIENNE: Listen to me. The daughters of Marshal Simon are also being detained here against their will. Take this ring and give it to M. Dagobert. He must go to my lawyer, Place Vendome No 7. I must go. Hurry.

MAYEUX: But Mademoiselle –

Scene 30

Rue Brise Miche.

MAYEUX: I have news, M. Dagobert. Rose and Blanche are in the convent of Ste Marie. And I have just seen Mlle de Cardoville. She is being detained in an asylum against her will.

DAGOBERT: We must go at once.

MAYEUX: Wait. Mlle de Cardoville gave me this ring. You must take it to her lawyer tomorrow.

DAGOBERT: Tomorrow will be too late.

MAYEUX: But why?

AGRICOLA: Where are you going, Father?

DAGOBERT: To rescue the children.

MAYEUX: They are heavily guarded, M. Dagobert.

DAGOBERT: I brought these children from the depths of Siberia to be at the Rue St Francois tomorrow. It is their dying mother's wish.

MAYEUX: No 3, the Rue St Francois?

DAGOBERT: How dost thou know the number?

MAYEUX: Earlier today Mlle de Cardoville's maid gave me a letter and a medal for safekeeping.

DAGOBERT: But this is exactly like the medal given to Rose and Blanche.

AGRICOLA: Mlle de Cardoville is their relation. She too must be at the Rue St Francois.

MAYEUX: And she does not even know.

DAGOBERT: We cannot wait for the wheels of justice to start turning.

AGRICOLA: No violence. We must appeal to the authorities.

DAGOBERT: When I tried to lay a charge against thy mother's confessor, the 'authorities' said they could do nothing and took your mother away.

AGRICOLA: But now there is proof, Father. Now we know where the girls are. The law is more powerful than all the Mother Superiors in the world.

DAGOBERT: There is no time.

AGRICOLA: Father –

DAGOBERT: You cannot stop me.

AGRICOLA: If you insist on going – then at least wait till it is dark.

DAGOBERT: I shall do this alone.

AGRICOLA: I am coming with thee.

MAYEUX: M. Dagobert. Agricola – it is dangerous.

FRANCOISE: Dagobert. Forgive me.

DAGOBERT: Francoise. Thank heavens. Please – do not kneel.

FRANCOISE: I beg thy forgiveness.

DAGOBERT: Why must I forgive thee?

AGRICOLA: Mother – thou art frozen.

FRANCOISE: Pardon me.

DAGOBERT: I accused thy confessor. Thou art not to blame.

MAYEUX: Come and sit down, Mme Francoise.

FRANCOISE: I prayed for mercy in prison. And God heard my prayers. I was released this morning.

AGRICOLA: Mayeux, pray make a fire.

MAYEUX: There is no charcoal left.

DAGOBERT: Francoise. Didst not tell me that when he first came to thee, Gabriel brought with him a bronze medal and some papers? And thou gavest them to thy confessor?

FRANCOISE: Yes, my dear.

AGRICOLA: Then Gabriel has the same interest as Marshal Simon's daughters and Mlle de Cardoville.

MAYEUX: They must all be at the Rue St Francois tomorrow.

DAGOBERT: They are all the victims of a conspiracy of wicked priests. I have never feared death, and yet those black robes strike terror in me.

FRANCOISE: Where art thou going?

MAYEUX: To rescue Rose and Blanche.

FRANCOISE: Thou canst not break into a convent. It is sacrilege.

DAGOBERT: I have made up my mind.

AGRICOLA: Mother, I shall go with him.

FRANCOISE: Alas, may heaven have pity on us.

Scene 31

Rue du Milieu-des-Ursins.

RODIN: On the 19th day of February 1682, the Reverend Father Provincial Alexander Bourdon wrote the following:

'His Majesty Louis XIV, in his Catholic goodness to our Order granted us the property of a Protestant convert, Marius de Rennepont, a relapsed heretic. He was condemned to the galleys, but escaped his punishment by committing suicide, for which terrible crime his body was thrown to the dogs. All his property has come to us; except for No 3 Rue St Francois and a sum of 50,000 gold crowns.

The house has been walled up for 150 years. At six tomorrow morning the masons will unblock the door.

ABBE: One more day. Are they all safely out of the way?

RODIN: They are. Jacques Rennepont, known as Couche-tout-nu, safely ensconced in the debtors' prison.

ABBE: He will not bother us tomorrow.

RODIN: The desmoiselles Rose and Blanche Simon are locked in separate cells in the convent.

ABBE: Nothing to fear there.

RODIN: Mlle de Cardoville is closely guarded.

ABBE: Good. The Indian Prince?

RODIN: I will deal with him.

ABBE: Excellent. Finally, there is the Abbé Gabriel.

RODIN: The young Abbé has been confined to the seminary.

ABBE: Gabriel will be the only representative present, the one rightful heir to this immense fortune. According to his act of renunciation, customary on taking Holy Orders, the fortune will therefore come to our Order. Tomorrow at 7 o'clock in the morning, you will conduct Gabriel to the Rue St Francois.

RODIN: I am at your command, M. L'Abbé.

Scene 32

The wind gusts.

The rain falls in torrents.

Dagobert and Agricola approach a small garden door in the convent wall.

The guards are making their rounds.

Their footsteps die away.

Agricola leans his shoulder against the door.

It is rotten.

The door gives way.

Scene 33

Rue du Milieu-des-Ursins

FARINGHEA: M. Rodin? You are M. Rodin?

RODIN: I am. Who are you?

FARINGHEA: I have a letter to deliver to you. In person. It is from India. You will recognise the writing as that of your contact in Pondicherry.

Rodin reaches out.

Faringhea holds the paper out of reach.

RODIN: You have a singular manner of delivering a letter in person. This is addressed to me.

FARINGHEA: But it is in my possession. I strangled a man and stole it.

RODIN: You strangled a man?

FARINGHEA: Swiftly, and silently.

RODIN: I am surprised at your frankness, Monsieur – what is your name?

FARINGHEA: Faringhea.

RODIN: M. Faringhea. May I have my letter?

FARINGHEA: Not yet.

RODIN: I see. What is it you want?

FARINGHEA: I have read the letter and I have found, brother, that you are like myself, a son of the good work.

RODIN: Good work.

FARINGHEA: The letter says: 'Obedience and courage, secrecy and patience, craft and audacity, union and devotion, these become us who have the world for our country, the brethren for our family, Rome for our queen.' My brothers also labour in many countries for the glory of Bohwanie.

RODIN: The glory of whom?

FARINGHEA: Bohwanie is our goddess. We are her sons.

RODIN: Who are these sons of Bohwanie, M. Faringhea?

FARINGHEA: Men of resolution, who sacrifice country and family. I have left India to fight for the success of the good work.

RODIN: And your aims?

FARINGHEA: The same as yours, brother. The greatest glory of your order is to make a corpse of man. Our work is also to make corpses of men. Man's death is sweet to Bohwanie.

RODIN: My order is concerned with the soul, the will, the mind, which must be disciplined.

FARINGHEA: You kill the soul and we the body. For what are bodies, deprived of soul, will, thought, but mere corpses? Take my hand, brother, Rome and Bohwanie are sisters.

RODIN: M. Faringhea, should you make corpses for love of your goddess, we should make you a head shorter for the love of another divinity called Justice. Now. Give me the letter.

FARINGHEA: M. Rodin, I am in Paris with a friend.

RODIN: M. Faringhea, I am not very interested in your private life.

FARINGHEA: I am in Paris with Prince Djalma. I knew that would interest you. We are in a house in the rue Blanche furnished by the generosity of Mlle de Cardoville. My master and I –

RODIN: You said Prince Djalma was your friend.

FARINGHEA: He is my master and my friend. Do you wish to hear more?

RODIN: Go on.

FARINGHEA: We sons of Bohwanie have a horror of shedding blood. We are

skilful. We have a powerful poison. By
letting a sleeper inhale a few grains of a
powder, we can induce a very deep sleep.
Opium is trash compared to this divine
narcotic.
    Yesterday Prince Djalma smoked his
usual pipe after dinner. He is still asleep. I
can leave him in his trance, or I can rouse
him. It depends on you.

RODIN: Now really, M. Faringhea. What a
story! Stolen letters, one man strangled,
another poisoned. You come from the
depths of India to Paris. You believe me
as great a scoundrel as yourself. I have
heard enough.

FARINGHEA: You recognise this medal?
I know that you wish to prevent the
Prince from being at a certain address
tomorrow. Say the word and Djalma will
be absent from the Rue St Francois.

RODIN: And if I do not oblige you?

FARINGHEA: I shall make sure Djalma is
there. We are brothers, you and I.

RODIN: Do not think you can compare
your insignificant ambitions with our
power.

FARINGHEA: It is up to you. You know
where to find me.

Scene 34

No 3, Rue St Francois.

A high wall.

Shaded by ancient trees.

Forty feet high.

A small door in one of the gates.

A vaulted passage.

Beyond the passage, an inner courtyard.

In the courtyard, a stone house.

The front door has been walled up.

The windows have been sealed with lead
plates.

The chimneys have been bricked up.

A mausoleum.

The night between the 12th and the 13th of
February is nearly at an end.

A large room, with walnut wainscotting,
black with age.

Ancient keys.

A deep, iron chest.

An intricate Florentine lock.

A large cedarwood casket.

Papers.

By the light of a copper lamp, the old
guardian, David Samuel, writes in a small
register.

Bathsheba, his wife, dictates to him from a
ledger.

Samuel is eighty-two years old.

He wears a long maroon dressing gown.

His wife, Bathsheba, is fifteen years
younger.

She is dressed in black.

A cap of starched lawn.

Like the headdress of a Dutch matron.

BATHSHEBA: Look, Samuel. The dawn.

SAMUEL: Come, Bathsheba. Our
    accounts must be in order before we
    deliver them to the rightful owners.

BATHSHEBA: At noon you will be
    delivered from a terrible responsibility.

SAMUEL: Bathsheba. Please check the
    summary of investments in the register. I
    will make sure that the bonds and
    vouchers are safe in the casket.

BATHSHEBA: God grant that M.
    Rennepont's heirs may be worthy of this
    royal fortune, and make noble use of it.

Scene 35

GABRIEL: Will you tell me, sir, why I have
    been unable to speak to his Reverence,
    the Abbé d'Aigrigny? And what is this
    place?

RODIN: You know.

GABRIEL: I do not know.

RODIN: What did your adopted mother
    say to you yesterday?

GABRIEL: I cannot tell you.

RODIN: The rules of our house state that
    you can have no secrets from your
    superiors.

GABRIEL: I have no secrets.

RODIN: You shut the door of your room yesterday.

GABRIEL: It was to a priest and not to her adopted son that Madame Baudoin wished to speak. I closed my door because I was to hear a confession.

RODIN: Welcome, M. l'Abbé.

ABBE: M. Rodin. My dear son. It has distressed me not to be able to speak to you sooner.

GABRIEL: M. l'Abbé –

ABBE: Please. I have something important to tell you. Twelve years ago, your adopted mother's confessor pointed out your astonishing ability at school. You were admitted into one of the Company's schools, and you received from our paternal care the benefits of a religious education.

GABRIEL: That is true, Father.

ABBE: You made rapid progress. Your resolution to take orders filled me with joy. I saw in you one of the future lights of our church. You wished to be a missionary. Though it was painful to part with our dear son, we could not refuse such a pious wish, and you were exemplary. What I am now about to say is confidential.

GABRIEL: Father, I am no longer entitled to your confidence.

ABBE: I cannot believe, my dear son, that there is any rift between us.

GABRIEL: Twelve years ago I entered the church school, loving, truthful and confiding. In three days, a credulous child, I was already a spy, remembering and reporting conversations to my Superior.

ABBE: My dear son, according to the rules, our Company may denounce each other without prejudice to love and mutual charity, and in the interests of our spiritual advancement.

GABRIEL: My childhood was spent in an atmosphere of terror, suspicion and restraint. For the words 'Love one another' you substituted 'Suspect one another'. There came a time when I could not feel devotion any more. It was then you told me that my adopted mother had but one desire.

ABBE: Indeed. That of seeing you take Holy Orders.

GABRIEL: I became a priest to please her. And the true spirit of Christ was so inspiring that gradually I became genuinely animated by the idea of practising His precepts. In my imagination a seminary was a holy place, where the love of humanity, tolerance and compassion were taught.

ABBE: Such is indeed the spirit of Christianity.

GABRIEL: Alas, Father, it was death and not life that I found thus so highly organised. I devoted myself to theological studies, full of messages of war, full of opposition to peace, progress and liberty.

ABBE: Theology is a buckler to protect the Catholic faith and a sword to combat heresy.

GABRIEL: Does not the gospel teach us to love one another? I read the casuists. Oh, Father, that was a new and dreadful revelation. On every page justification for robbery, calumny, adultery, perjury, murder, regicide. When I considered that I, a priest of the God of love, was to belong to a Company whose leaders gloried in such doctrines, I made a solemn oath to break forever the ties which bound me. I beg you to release me from my vows.

RODIN: Release you?

ABBE: Let me be clear about this. Are you determined to leave the Company?

GABRIEL: It will be painful, Father, but I must. I wish to obtain a village curacy. I can do good there.

ABBE: Very well, then. If you are really sure.

GABRIEL: Then, Father, you release me from my vows?

ABBE: I have not the power to do so. But I will write to Rome.

GABRIEL: Thank you, Father.

ABBE: You were poor and an orphan. We stretched out our arms to you. I shall pray for you.

GABRIEL: Father, I am not ungrateful.

ABBE: Now that I understand your real motives, of course it is my duty to release

you from your vows. Your adopted
mother told you that you were soon to
receive a large inheritance.

GABRIEL: My adopted mother spoke to
me only of her conscience.

RODIN: To put it plainly, you are violating
your oath because you wish to take back
your gift.

GABRIEL: What gift? What are you
talking about?

ABBE: M. Rodin, you go too far. Our dear
son could only have acted in the base
manner you suggest had he known about
his inheritance. But he affirms the
contrary.

GABRIEL: Heaven is my witness: this is
the first I have heard of any inheritance.

RODIN: One of your paternal ancestors
left a will that is to be read today, at noon,
in this house. Clearly the anticipation of a
fortune has changed your sentiments, and
you wish to be free to reclaim your
inheritance.

GABRIEL: You think me infamous
enough to break my word in the hope of
possessing a modest patrimony? I freely
resigned my property to you once, and I
do so again now.

RODIN: But you could change your mind
tomorrow.

ABBE: I suggest you write down your
intentions. When the notary arrives to
read the will, he can witness this
document. Everything must be done
properly.

GABRIEL: Very well. I voluntarily renew
the donation made by me to the Company
of Jesus. Any property which may
hereafter belong to me, whatever its
value, I make over to them. Gabriel de
Rennepont.

Scene 36

The house is unbricked.

Samuel advances with his keys.

He unlocks the door.

The door opens.

A current of damp, cold air.

The old man shudders.

A pair of folding doors.

Deep-fringed damask curtains.

Deep purple.

A deep Turkish carpet.

Deep armchairs of gilded wood.

Heavy chandeliers.

A round table.

A crimson velvet cloth.

SAMUEL: The will is to be read in the Red
Salon. I am ready, gentlemen. Please,
enter. The moment is come.

PART TWO

Scene 37

Gabriel, Rodin, Father d'Aigrigny, Bathsheba and the Notary stand round the table.

NOTARY: M. Gabriel Francois Marie de Rennepont, priest, are you the only descendant of the Rennepont family here present?

GABRIEL: I believe I am.

The notary draws the will from its envelope.

NOTARY: I shall now read the last will and testament of M. Marius de Rennepont, dated the 13th of February, 1682.

MARIUS: On the 13th February, 1832, at ten o'clock precisely, the Red Salon at No 3 Rue St Francois will be opened to my heirs. After my will has been read, the inheritance will be divided equally amongst those of my kindred who are there in person.

My grandfather was a lay Catholic who joined the Company of Jesus. In 1610 he became a Protestant. My father was then subject to the Company's violent hatred and since then my family has been mercilessly persecuted.

RODIN: Get to the will.

MARIUS: This morning I sent for Isaac Samuel. I have entrusted him with 50,000 crowns. He will invest the above sum for my heirs and allow it to accumulate for 150 years, into a royal fortune. My most earnest desire is that my family should unite and put into practice the divine words 'Love one another'.

If it be heaven's will that they are passionate souls, compassionate towards those who suffer, to the work of darkness, restraint and despotism, my family will oppose light and liberty. This house is to serve as a meeting place for my descendants, to carry out my last wishes.

NOTARY: This 13th day of February, 1682.

MARIUS: Marius de Rennepont.

GABRIEL: Alas, his great idea can never be realised now.

SAMUEL: Here is the key to the register. In it you will find the exact statement of the sums derived from the investment entrusted to my grandfather.

BATHSHEBA: Here is the casket.

RODIN: What is the sum total? The amount.

BATHSHEBA: Begin, my dear.

SAMUEL: Debit. Two million francs per annum, at five per cent.

Thirty-nine million eight hundred thousand francs.

Nine hundred thousand francs ditto, at three per cent.

Twenty-two million two hundred and seventy-five thousand francs.

Five thousand shares in the Bank of France bought at one franc ninety.

Nine million five hundred thousand francs.

Three million three hundred and forty-five thousand francs.

A hundred and twenty-five ducats of Neopolitan rents.

Nine million twenty thousand francs.

Five thousand Austrian metallics of a thousand florins.

Eleven million six hundred and twenty-five thousand francs.

Seventy-five thousand pounds sterling per annum at three per cent.

Fifty-five million four hundred and sixty-eight, seven hundred and fifty thousand francs.

One million two hundred thousand Dutch florins at two and a half per cent.

Sixty million six hundred and six thousand francs.

Cash in banknotes, gold and silver.

Five hundred and thirty-five thousand two hundred and fifty francs.

SAMUEL: Total. Two hundred and twelve million, one hundred and seventy-five thousand francs.

BATHSHEBA: We hold securities for this amount.

RODIN: 212 million?

ABBE: What did you say?

BATHSHEBA: After 150 years, the 50,000 crowns have yielded two hundred and twelve million, one hundred and seventy-five thousand francs.

GABRIEL: These riches might have belonged to me.

ABBE: My dear son, the poor will bless you.

RODIN: Let us thank Providence for so much wealth devoted to the glory of the Lord.

NOTARY: In the name of the law, I declare that Gabriel de Rennepont is the sole heir to the estate, bequeathed under the said will. Which estate the said Gabriel de Rennepont, priest, has freely and voluntarily made over by deed of gift to Frederic Emmanuel de Baudeville, Marquis d'Aigrigny, priest, who has accepted the same and is therefore the only legal owner of the property by virtue of the deed signed in my presence by the said Gabriel de Rennepont and Frederic d'Aigrigny

Dagobert appears.

Almost fainting.

His left arm is in a sling.

He leans on Agricola.

GABRIEL: My brother, my father. Heaven has sent you.

ABBE: Who are you, sir?

DAGOBERT: You do not recognise me, Colonel D'Aigrigny.

ABBE: No, sir.

DAGOBERT: I accuse you of robbing Marshal Simon's daughters, and Gabriel Rennepont and Mlle de Cardoville of their rightful inheritance. They are thy relations, my boy, as is Mlle de Cardoville.

GABRIEL: I have cheated them out of their inheritance.

DAGOBERT: Thou wilt share the money with them.

GABRIEL: But I have made my share over to another.

DAGOBERT: To another?

GABRIEL: To this gentleman.

DAGOBERT: That devil?

GABRIEL: I am a minister in a religion which honours poverty. But I will not see others wronged. The last will of a dying man was to bequeath an evangelic mission to his descendants. This mission shall be accomplished, even if I have to cancel the donation I have made.

RODIN: Your deed of gift is a legal document.

GABRIEL: It is true. And I made the donation freely.

NOTARY: I witnessed the deed.

AGRICOLA: But Gabriel could only give what belonged to him. He never supposed you would use him to rob other people.

ABBE: The Abbé Gabriel was the only heir present..

NOTARY: All I can do is execute the will. If you wish to take the matter further –

GABRIEL: M. l'Abbé, will you be content with my portion of the property, and agree to place the rest in safe hands till the other heirs can prove their claim?

ABBE: It is not my personal concern, but that of our pious institution. We can make no concessions.

RODIN: M. Notary, please explain to the Abbé Gabriel that the civil code is much less easy to violate than a mere religious oath. Is it not so?

NOTARY: Yes, sir.

Samuel produces a sealed envelope.

Rodin takes the casket and tries to leave.

SAMUEL: One moment, sir.

ABBE: What is it?

SAMUEL: A codicil to the will.

RODIN: I protest.

NOTARY: Gentlemen. The codicil adjourns the implementation of the will to June 1st, 1832.

AGRICOLA: There is hope.

MARIUS: In the event of any suspicious circumstances, or the possibility of fraudulent practices, the trustees may, at their discretion, activate the codicil. If this should happen, the house will be closed again and the funds left in the hands of the trustees. 13th February 1682. Marius de Rennepont.

ABBE: A forgery.

NOTARY: The signature is identical to that on the will. It is, of course, open to you to dispute the authenticity of the codicil.

Rodin's nails are full of blood.

AGRICOLA: Three and a half months to establish the true claim.

GABRIEL: We have nothing more to fear.

Samuel takes the casket.

Scene 38

PRINCESS: 212 million. With such resources, the Company could have dominated the whole of France.

ABBE: It is enough to drive one mad with rage.

PRINCESS: Is there no hope?

ABBE: Only if Gabriel does not revoke his own donation. That alone amounts to more than thirty million.

PRINCESS: But that is what we originally anticipated. Why despair?

ABBE: Because Gabriel is bound to be encouraged by his family to try to annul the gift. Rodin, we must inform Rome.

Rodin bows.

ABBE: Write: Our hopes have been defeated. The Rennepont inheritance is lost. I did everything possible to secure our rights.

RODIN: No. The man is mad.

ABBE: Continue, please.

RODIN: Our positions are to be reversed, M. l'Abbé.

Rodin draws a paper from his pocket. The Abbé presses the paper to his lips. He returns it to Rodin with a bow.

ABBE: I see that you now have the right to command me.

RODIN: I have kept Rome closely informed of the progress of this affair. I have described your tactics to them. And I have told them of your signal lack of success. This affair has over-stretched your abilities.

ABBE: But surely, had it not been for the codicil –

RODIN: What have you achieved? The daughters of General Simon shut up in a convent. Adrienne de Cardoville confined. Couche-tout-nu in prison. Everything has been mechanical, fraught with risk and dependent on physical violence. Violence breeds violence. We are skilful men, we see in the dark. We do not brawl in daylight.

ABBE: Sir, you are too severe.

RODIN: Once you were a fine military officer, irresistible to women. Now you are worn out. Exhausted. You lack the concentration necessary for real power. I, on the other hand, am totally devoted to the Company. I am ugly, dirty, unloved and unloving. I have all my manhood about me. Intact.

ABBE: But the family now know of one another's existence.

RODIN: I mean to bring the whole of this 212 million into the coffers of the Company.

ABBE: Impossible.

RODIN: If this money falls into the hands of the Rennepont family, think of the forces that would rally round them. Marshal Simon, the man of the people. Gabriel, the apostle of democracy in the church. Adrienne de Cardoville, priestess of elegance, grace and beauty. Agricola Baudoin, a plebian in heart, a poet in imagination. Prince Djalma, chivalrous, bold, as implacable in his hate as in his affections. Even a degenerate like Couche-tout-nu will be purified by contact with these generous natures.

ABBE: And what can you do that I have not?

RODIN: You have manipulated external circumstances. We must act upon these people's passions. Tell me, do people die of despair?

ABBE: Yes.

RODIN: May not an excess of sensuality lead to death, in a slow, voluptuous agony?

ABBE: Yes.

RODIN: If you, once an impious, debauched man of the world, could be converted to priesthood – then a good family can as easily by converted to its opposite. Besides, we have a powerful ally, whose presence will render them still more vulnerable.

PRINCESS: What ally?

RODIN: An ally who can decimate a population.

ABBE: Who is this ally?

RODIN: The cholera. Write.

ABBE: I am ready.

Scene 39

Rodin unseals a letter.

He contemplates the picture of a swineherd dressed in rags.

Beneath the boy the Papal emblems surround the head of an old man.

The picture is called 'The Prediction'. The youth of Pope Sixtus V.

RODIN: 'He shall be Pope'.

He opens the letter.

RODIN: We must enrage philosophers all over Europe. We must make liberalism foam at the mouth. We must raise the strongest objections to Rome, and proclaim these three propositions to the world:
1. It is obscene to claim that the people may be saved, whatever their faith, if their morals be pure. 2. It is absurd to grant liberty of conscience to the people. 3. Freedom of the press must be deplored. The weak will declare these propositions orthodox. Then the storm will break. A general revolt against Rome, a wide schism. The sacred college divided against itself. Let there be pillage, rape, massacre. Rivers of blood. Finally, the Pope will abdicate. The Rennepont inheritance will pay for the election. I shall be Pope.

Scene 40

DOCTOR: Your complexion is less flushed.

ADRIENNE: I hope they are paying you well for this.

DOCTOR: Still this delusion that you do not need my care?

ADRIENNE: I shall go to law.

DOCTOR: I beg you not to. Remember, there are other people involved.

ADRIENNE: My aunt and the Abbé d'Aigrigny.

DOCTOR: No, Mademoiselle. I mean the two men who tried to break into the convent, Agricola Baudoin and his father. We have not reported them to the police. If you lodge a complaint, their nocturnal escapade will be revealed.

ADRIENNE: I see.

NURSE: There are two gentlemen to see you, Mademoiselle. One of them says he is a magistrate.

ADRIENNE: Heaven be praised.

DOCTOR: Take care, Mademoiselle. Remember. The fate of the soldier and his son is in your hands.

Rodin.

A man dressed in black.

MAGISTRATE: I am M. de Guernande. You are Doctor Baleinier? A charge of medical malpractice has been laid against you.

DOCTOR: You insult me.

MAGISTRATE: Mademoiselle, is it true that you were tricked into coming here?

ADRIENNE: I am not sure – that I wish to press charges.

DOCTOR: It is true. Mademoiselle was tricked into coming here.

MAGISTRATE: You admit it, then?

DOCTOR: Certainly. We are often obliged to employ such means when persons who most need our assistance are unconscious of their own sad state.

MAGISTRATE: You have been charged with confining Mlle de Cardoville against her will, for financial gain.

DOCTOR: Who accuses me?

RODIN: I do.

DOCTOR: You?But I beg Mlle de Cardoville to confirm that only this morning I told her that she was greatly improved.

RODIN: Mademoiselle never lost her reason.

DOCTOR: I maintain that she did lose it. I also maintain that she is not yet fully cured, and I wash my hands of all future responsibility.

ADRIENNE: May I leave, then?

DOCTOR: Mademoiselle is perfectly free to go whenever she wishes. Excuse me.

He leaves.

ADRIENNE: At last, thanks to you, sir, I am free. How can I ever repay you?

RODIN: Come, come. We will talk about gratitude later. M. de Guernande?

MAGISTRATE: Of course. Excuse me.

He leaves.

RODIN: The magistrate has gone to fetch the daughters of Marshal Simon. Perhaps you would agree to take charge of these innocent young girls?

ADRIENNE: But of course. You are so kind, sir –

RODIN: Do you know the real motive for your imprisonment in this house?

ADRIENNE: Mme de St Dizier's hatred of me.

RODIN: And a desire to rob you of an immense fortune. You and the daughters of Marshal Simon were due to have been present at the reading of the will of one of your ancestors, on February the 13th. Those not present in person forfeited their claim to any inheritance. There are other heirs, too. A young Indian prince.

ADRIENNE: Prince Djalma?

RODIN: Thrown into the midst of Paris, with his ardour and innocence.

ADRIENNE: I have helped him – secretly – through his servant, a good man called Faringhea.

RODIN: Have you met the Prince?

ADRIENNE: Not yet. I would so like to know that he is safe. Please, be so good as to tell me your name.

RODIN: I am M. Rodin. A mere scribe who records the ideas of others.

ADRIENNE: M. Rodin.

RODIN: Formerly secretary to the Abbé d'Aigrigny. Now without employment, but no matter. I am glad to be free of the influence of the Abbé, one of the cleverest and most dangerous men I have known.

ADRIENNE: How did you learn I was here?

RODIN: On the 12th of February, the Abbé delivered a report to me –

ADRIENNE: My interview with Mme de St Dizier?

RODIN: The same. As I read, I was overcome with delight and enthusiasm. Your ideas are quite brilliant. I tried to convince the Abbé d'Aigrigny of his error. You were clearly not mad. I began to connect other pieces of information, until I united all the threads of the plot against your family. I went straight to the magistrate.

ADRIENNE: How is it that with your undoubted merits you were so humbly employed?

RODIN: Indolence, my dear. A horror of taking moral responsibility. I was the happiest man in the world. I trusted the Abbé: his thoughts, his wishes, became mine. After work, I returned to my poor garret, lit a fire, dined on vegetables.

ADRIENNE: Had you no ambition?

RODIN: For what?

ADRIENNE: Well, for a certain degree of comfort, perhaps.

RODIN: I require only warm clothes, a good stove, a good mattress, a good piece of bread, a good radish flavoured with good grey salt, and some good clear water. For that, my twelve hundred francs a year have more than sufficed.

ADRIENNE: And yet you decided to help me and my family.

RODIN: I understand the noble pride with which you contemplate the mob of vain, ridiculous men who look upon woman as a creature destined for their service.

ADRIENNE: You understand me so well.

RODIN: Why should our convictions not be the same?
    You had nothing in common with those hypocritical jealous minds. You live for

the noblest aims that could tempt a lofty soul.

ADRIENNE: It is a delight to hear a man of your superior intellect praise me. Your devotion to me and my family has been exemplary. I insist on expressing my gratitude. After all, it is on my account that you are now unemployed.

RODIN: There is no need, Mademoiselle.

MAYEUX: Mademoiselle.

ADRIENNE: La Mayeux. M. Rodin, this is the adopted sister of the gallant young man who tried to rescue me from this house. She is a rare creature. La Mayeux – you must not weep.

MAYEUX: You are so good, Mademoiselle.

ADRIENNE: She has a good heart.

RODIN: She has a noble heart. This girl showed great courage in rejecting the shameful wages offered by the Mother Superior. She was asked to spy on her employer.

ADRIENNE: Why, that is infamous.

MAYEUX: How do you know?

RODIN: And is not your adopted brother Agricola Baudoin, the gallant workman, the popular poet?

MAYEUX: Monsieur –

ADRIENNE: The least praise embarrasses her.

MAYEUX: Excuse me, Mademoiselle, I am not accustomed to such kindness.

ADRIENNE: Kindness? I have set my heart on having you for a friend and it shall be so. I can give you employment, if you wish.

MAYEUX: Are you free to go, Mademoiselle?

ADRIENNE: I am, thanks to this kind man. And so are Marshal Simon's daughters.

MAYEUX: Rose and Blanche? Oh, Mademoiselle – M. Dagobert will be so happy.

DAGOBERT: At last.

Dagobert seizes Rodin by the collar.

ADRIENNE: In the name of heaven, sir, what are you doing?

DAGOBERT: I am trying to persuade this wretch to tell me where my children are.

RODIN: Let go.

MAYEUX: M. Dagobert –

RODIN: Help.

ADRIENNE: Have mercy, sir, listen to him.

MAYEUX: M. Dagobert, this is Mlle de Cardoville.

DAGOBERT: I beg your pardon, Mademoiselle.

ADRIENNE: What has this gentleman done to you?

DAGOBERT: The children must be restored to me.

RODIN: They will be, I assure you.

DAGOBERT: If Mademoiselle were not here, I would –

RODIN: Take this, sir, before you judge me.

DAGOBERT: My cross.

He kisses the cross.

DAGOBERT: My most precious possession. This cross is my relic. It was given to me by a saint, a hero.

RODIN: Did the great Napoleon really give this to you himself?

DAGOBERT: Yes, sir.

RODIN: Blessed be my hand for having restored you this glorious treasure.

ADRIENNE: This good man is most concerned to restore the children to you.

RODIN: You shall have your angels back again.

DAGOBERT: Is this true? Then I must apologise to you, sir. I was wrong to abuse you.

Dagobert holds out his hand. Rodin presses it.

ADRIENNE: M. Dagobert, a magistrate has gone to fetch Marshal Simon's daughters.

RODIN: The Marshal will have to demand an explanation from the Abbé d'Aigrigny for persecuting his daughters.

DAGOBERT: How so?

RODIN: Do you think it was mere chance that brought about the event at the Inn of the White Falcon?

DAGOBERT: How could the Abbé know that I and the children were travelling through Leipzig?

RODIN: You were robbed of your papers and your cross by Morok. He sent them to the Abbé.

ADRIENNE: Does the Abbé have spies everywhere?

RODIN: Do not question me.

ADRIENNE: What do you fear, sir?

RODIN: Have you ever heard of a powerful association that extends its net over the whole world, and has disciples in every class of society?

ADRIENNE: What association?

RODIN: Your ignorance astonishes me.

ADRIENNE: Why?

RODIN: Because you lived with your aunt and must often have seen the Abbé d'Aigrigny. Mme de St Dizier owes her formidable influence to this association.

DAGOBERT: What is its name?

RODIN: The Company of Jesus.

ADRIENNE: The Jesuits. Why, they only exist in books.

RODIN: These people are powerful. Their animosity is terrible. The master of this house is one of the Company's most devoted lay members.

ADRIENNE: Dr Baleinier?

RODIN: He is but a blind instrument of the Abbe d'Aigrigny, the most formidable leader of that most formidable Company. They can corrupt your closest friends if they are really determined.

Marshal Simon.

A tall man in a blue frock coat.

A broad forehead.

Short, grey hair.

A man of the people.

A man of action.

Rodin disappears.

SIMON: My friend. My old friend. Where are they? My wife? My child? Are they not with thee?

DAGOBERT: My friend –

ADRIENNE: Marshal Simon. I am Mlle de Cardoville, a relation of yours and your children.

SIMON: Children?

ADRIENNE: Twin daughters –

SIMON: Two daughters? I find three loved beings instead of two. Mademoiselle, pity my impatience. Where are they?

DAGOBERT: General, I returned from Siberia alone with your two daughters.

SIMON: And Eva?

DAGOBERT: I set out the day after her death.

SIMON: I thought I had a right to happiness after so many years of suffering. I must see the children.

ADRIENNE: Marshall, I hope you may see them very soon.

SIMON: Where are they?

DAGOBERT: While I was away from home, my wife's confessor persuaded her that your daughters would be better in a convent.

SIMON: Then let us go to them.

DAGOBERT: The convent will not allow anyone to see them.

SIMON: You have betrayed me.

ADRIENNE: Marshal, do not blame him. He risked his life to rescue your children.

Rodin appears with Rose and Blanche.

ADRIENNE: I was not deceived.

ROSE: Dagobert –

DAGOBERT: Children, this is your father.

BLANCHE: Father –

Simon turns round.

His daughters throw themselves into his arms.

DAGOBERT: You have saved me.

MAYEUX: Bless you, sir.

ADRIENNE: Come and meet the Marshal, M. Rodin. You are a good man.

RODIN: Providence, my dear young lady, does not trouble itself with the good it has done, but with the good that remains to be done. The Abbé d'Aigrigny is unmasked, you are free, the brave soldier has recovered his cross. La Mayeux is sure of a protectress, the Marshal has his children. I have my share in all these joys. My heart is satisfied. Adieu, my friends.

Scene 41

The Rue Blanche.

A circular apartment.

Hung with Indian drapery.

Perfumes.

Persian tobacco.

Faringhea feeds the golden bowl of a hookah.

Its tube, like a serpent, held by Djalma.

A cashmere robe, fastened with an orange shawl.

His eyes.

Like black diamonds set in mother of pearl.

A slow breath half opens his rosy lips.

A spiral of smoke, freshly scented with rosewater.

Scene 42

The Rue d'Anjou.

A new temple dedicated to the worship of beauty.

Hung with white silk.

Waves of white muslin billow from the ceiling.

Ivory doors.

Inlaid with mother of pearl.

A white marble mantelpiece.

An ermine carpet.

A low bed.

Cambric sheets.

Trimmed with lace.

A white silk mattress.

Lace.

Cambric.

White silk.

Adrienne is in bed.

Her soft, dark eyes gaze at a basket of red camellias.

Her smiling lips are moist and rosy.

Scene 41a

DJALMA: The old man with the good heart is late.

FARINGHEA: He will return. He gave his word. Some more tobacco?

DJALMA: No.

FARINGHEA: You are restless, my lord.

DJALMA: I am impatient to see Paris.

FARINGHEA: It will not be long now.

Scene 42a

ADRIENNE: I am free. I am alone. When will I find the man who shares my dreams?

Scene 41b

FARINGHEA: Soon this land of enchantment will be yours. And the French women, the Parisian beauties, are miracles of elegance and grace. On a warm evening, surrounded by flowers and perfumes, the exquisite creatures float in softly-lit rooms. At the end of an avenue, in a sheet of golden light, I see white sylph-like forms, voluptuous phantoms, throwing you kisses from the tips of their rosy fingers.

DJALMA: To ask for purity from a woman one must be as chaste as she.

FARINGHEA: With civilised people, my lord, the man who marries in innocence is ridiculed.

DJALMA: So, like our sultans, civilised men require of women the innocence they have themselves lost?

FARINGHEA: The less they have of it, my lord, the more they require it.

DJALMA: A pure and virgin love mingled in two hearts is like two drops of dew blending in the centre of a flower.

Scene 42b

ADRIENNE: A young tiger, proud, wild, handsome, perhaps, with untamed passions, encountering the sophistication of a refined society. What will Prince Djalma think of me? Dare I meet him? Could he be – no. He is not my hero. I have no wish to civilise him. And yet –

Scene 41c

FARINGHEA: You shall enjoy all the voluptuous pleasures of Paris, Prince Djalma.

DJALMA: Thy words burn into me like poison. These women do not exist. And even if they did – they would not look at me. I am – a barbarian.

FARINGHEA: For that very reason you will have Parisian women at your feet. Treat them as you like – be tender, be fierce – let a cry of rage be heard between kisses – they will be terrified and charmed. They will fall at your feet, palpitating with fear and desire. You will be their god.

Scene 42c

MAYEUX: Mademoiselle. You are betrayed.

ADRIENNE: I do not understand you.

MAYEUX: This morning I visited my sister. On my way back, I saw M. Rodin near the Hotel de St. Dizier. He was talking most earnestly to the Abbé d'Aigrigny. They are plotting together, I am sure of it.

ADRIENNE: We must not be too hasty. Remember, M. Rodin released me from Dr. Baleinier's asylum. He restored Marshal Simon's daughters.

MAYEUX: But if he has so much reason to hate the Abbé, why should they meet?

ADRIENNE: Well – remember, the Abbé fears M. Rodin. Perhaps he sought him out to beg for mercy.

MAYEUX: It is possible. And yet, believe me, Mademoiselle. I am sure you are deceived.

FLORINE: Mademoiselle, I have just been at the Hotel de St. Dizier. I was leaving the pavilion, when I saw M. Rodin coming out of the main house.

MAYEUX: There, Mademoiselle, you see? He must have been visiting the Princess.

ADRIENNE: Where did he go, Florine?

FLORINE: He got into a hackney coach and ordered the man to drive to the Rue Blanche.

MAYEUX: He is betraying you and the Prince.

FLORINE: If I might suggest –

ADRIENNE: Please.

FLORINE: When I was superintending the arrangements for Prince Djalma in the Rue Blanche, I always entered through the conservatory. I still have my key. The Prince often sits in a little salon near the conservatory. You could overhear his conversation with M. Rodin.

ADRIENNE: Florine, I could never spy on anyone.

FLORINE: I beg your pardon, Mademoiselle. But it may be your only chance to clarify the matter.

MAYEUX: Mlle Florine is right. It is the only way to resolve your suspicions.

ADRIENNE: I suppose so. It would be weakness not to be on my guard.

FLORINE: We must hurry, Mademoiselle.

Scene 41d

Adrienne and Florine enter the greenhouse.

RODIN: My dear Prince. I have come to open your cage for you.

DJALMA: May I go out? To see Paris?

RODIN: Now that you have grown used to the Parisian air, in the safety of your own house, your benefactor feels you may venture further afield.

DJALMA: Let us go immediately. I wish to thank him.

RODIN: In due course, my dear Prince. He wishes to remain unknown.

DJALMA: How can that be? A man of honour should not conceal his friendship.

RODIN: Suppose a woman were concerned?

DJALMA: A woman.

RODIN: Your benefactress is a woman. A noble matron of intelligence and sensitivity.

DJALMA: Ah. She is old. Why may I not meet her then?

RODIN: She has her reasons. Be assured, she has the chivalry of a man and the dignity of a woman.

DJALMA: Then I must respect her desire for secrecy.

RODIN: In three months time you will come into your full inheritance. You will be able to appear in the best houses in Paris, in a manner becoming the son of a king. Then, should you wish, you may repay your benefactress.

DJALMA: In her place I would have done the same. I can accept such generosity from a mother.

RODIN: I must warn you that when you do go out into society, you may well discover enemies who are jealous of your great wealth.

DJALMA: I shall kill them.

RODIN: Here one does not kill one's enemies. Here society examines, judges, and if there is good reason, punishes.

DJALMA: In my quarrels I am both judge and executioner.

FARINGHEA: A letter from the Abbé d'Aigrigny, M. Rodin. He expects an immediate reply.

RODIN: It must be important. Please excuse me. Oh dear. How vexing.

DJALMA: What is the matter?

RODIN: I seem to have forgotten my glasses. How annoying.

DJALMA: Shall I read it for you, Father?

RODIN: I could not impose – no, it is out of the question. And yet – if you could – I would be so obliged –

DJALMA: Allow me. 'M. Rodin. Your visit this morning to the Hotel de St Dizier can only be considered as a new act of aggression. You will receive a pension of one thousand francs a month on condition you leave Paris immediately. I expect your agreement by return. If you do not reply by four o'clock this afternoon, then war will be declared between us.'

RODIN: The Abbé d'Aigrigny.

Rodin takes the letter and tears it in half and crumples it.

RODIN: This is my reply.

A sound from the greenhouse.

Djalma and Adrienne see each other.

DJALMA: This is a dream.

ADRIENNE: Monsieur –

RODIN: You here, Mademoiselle?

DJALMA: Who is she?

ADRIENNE: I am Adrienne de Cardoville. I hope you will continue to accept from a sister the hospitality that you did not refuse from a mother. M. Rodin, I came here to spy on you. But I see now that you are no friend of the Abbé d'Aigrigny. I have stooped to deceit for the first time in my life. I owe you an apology.

DJALMA: Mlle de Cardoville?

RODIN: Your secret benefactress.

DJALMA: But how can this be?

ADRIENNE: I must go.

DJALMA: Please. Stay. I have waited so long. I must talk to you.

ADRIENNE: I cannot speak to you.

DJALMA: When shall I see you again?

ADRIENNE: I do not know. I cannot say. I must leave. Come, Florine.

Adrienne goes.

Rodin detains Florine for a moment.

Djalma weeps.

RODIN: If I led you to believe she was old, it was to protect you. At your age it is too easy to fall in love.

DJALMA: I have fallen in love, M. Rodin.

RODIN: My dear Prince. Prepare yourself for disappointment. Your beautiful protectress loves another. A handsome young man. A poet.

Djalma utters a cry of savage grief.

RODIN: Come, you must not give way. Remember, how eager you were to see Paris? Come, my dear Prince, be of good cheer.

Scene 43

MAYEUX: My own room. A thick carpet. The clock ticks softly. The wood crackles in the fire. I have never been so happy.

Scene 44

La Mayeux's room.

Florine's satin shoes scarcely touch the carpet.

She places the candle on the mantelpiece.

She opens a shabby trunk.

She finds a journal.

In its place she leaves an envelope.

Scene 43a

AGRICOLA: Good morning, dear La Mayeux.

MAYEUX: Good morning, Agricola.

AGRICOLA: How good it is to see thee so warm and comfortable.

MAYEUX: Come. Sit down.

AGRICOLA: I have so much to tell thee. My mother has gone with Gabriel to his new curacy in the country.

Scene 44a

FLORINE: 'My cheek burned beneath his fraternal kiss. I felt proud that I was so well dressed. Did he notice my clothes, my hair?'

Scene 43b

AGRICOLA: Mayeux – thou knowest that I have always confided in thee.

MAYEUX: I know,

AGRICOLA: Well – perhaps not always. I have never spoken to thee of my heart. About love. About – my love affairs.

MAYEUX: I know.

AGRICOLA: Mayeux – I think I am falling in love.

Scene 44b

FLORINE: 'He entered, embraced me and spoke of falling in love.'

Scene 43c

AGRICOLA: It is someone I have known for a long time. I have not told her of my love. I do not know if I should tell her.

MAYEUX: Why should you not tell her?

AGRICOLA: She may think of me just as a friend, a brother almost. She may not share my feelings.

MAYEUX: Is she beautiful?

AGRICOLA: Very beautiful.

MAYEUX: I see.

AGRICOLA: Should I tell her?

MAYEUX: It is for you to decide, Agricola.

AGRICOLA: Perhaps I should not burden you with such questions.

Scene 44c

FLORINE: 'Agricola loves another and cannot even bring himself to tell me her name.'

Scene 43d

MAYEUX: 'He could never have loved me, a hunchback. I was a fool to hope.'

Scene 44d

FLORINE: 'I must find the resignation of a saint, who loves and suffers and does not hope.'

Scene 43e

A high wind.

A single candle.

MAYEUX: A bank note for five hundred francs. 'Your journal will be a great success. The story of a hunchback's love for a working-class hero. Agricola will be so touched when he learns of it. We enclose five hundred francs that you may not be without resources, should you shrink from the congratulations which will certainly overwhelm you by tomorrow, when your journal is published.' I cannot stay here.

Scene 44e

Florine returns to La Mayeux's room.

She sees the shabby trunk, open and empty.

FLORINE: It is too late to return the journal.

Scene 45

RODIN: My dear Mlle de Cardoville. La Mayeux owned nothing and yet five hundred francs was found in her room. You loaded her with favours, yet she leaves your house without explaining why. Remember what I told you about a certain Company? I draw no conclusions, my dear young lady, but may I suggest that you have escaped some great danger. Your obedient humble servant, Rodin.

Scene 46

FLORINE: Mademoiselle, you look sad.

ADRIENNE: I am thinking about La Mayeux. But I am not sad really. After all, I am free.

FLORINE: Free – but unhappy.

ADRIENNE: What makes you think I am unhappy?

FLORINE: You are alone so much. You occupy yourself with books about other countries. 'Travels in India'. 'Letters from India.'

ADRIENNE: Surely it is not so strange that I should be interested in India. After all, I have a cousin who comes from that country.

FLORINE: And from whom you ran away. And whom you will not see.

ADRIENNE: We cannot meet, Florine.

FLORINE: But why? He loves you, Mademoiselle, with all the ardour of a first love.

ADRIENNE: He loves me?

FLORINE: He loves you to distraction. He is in despair because he thinks you love another. I heard M. Rodin tell him.

ADRIENNE: Indeed.

FLORINE: You must see him again, Mademoiselle.

ADRIENNE: I cannot. What could I say? I was spying on him.

FLORINE: You can see him in India.

ADRIENNE: I fear you have been reading my books, Florine.

FLORINE: Mademoiselle – tonight he will be at the theatre. You may see him there and be quite safe.

ADRIENNE: Florine, thank you. Tonight I shall go to the theatre.

M. Rodin enters

RODIN: Mademoiselle.

ADRIENNE: Pray, sir, draw near. You are the best of friends and the declared enemy of all lies. Your perception is remarkable.

RODIN: You flatter me.

ADRIENNE: You have read the depths of a woman's heart. You told Prince Djalma that I was in love. I love the Prince. I am indebted to you.

RODIN: There is some mistake. I have never spoken of the sentiments that you entertain for Prince Djalma.

ADRIENNE: No. You told the Prince that I loved someone else. And you knew of his passion for me. Let the sight of our happiness be your only punishment for lying to him.

RODIN: I was trying to protect you.

ADRIENNE: La Mayeux was generously devoted to me. She disappeared mysteriously, and you have done your best to cast suspicion on her. Prince Djalma has a deep affection for me, and you try to stifle that sentiment.

RODIN: Mademoiselle, you are forgetting the services I have rendered.

ADRIENNE: I do not deny, sir, that you took me away from Dr Baleinier's asylum. But the law would have released me sooner or later.

RODIN: You were drowning and I saved you. Doubtless someone else would have saved you another day.

ADRIENNE: A lunatic asylum is not a river. M. Rodin, let me give you a piece of advice.

RODIN: Good advice is always an excellent thing.

ADRIENNE: In India travellers keep great fires burning to frighten away the poisonous snakes which come out at night. For a while I was your dupe, and I tell you without hate, without anger, that I look upon you from today as a dangerous enemy. However, I do not fear you. There is something stronger than you and yours: a woman's resolve to defend her happiness.

RODIN: My dear young lady. I am your very humble servant.

Scene 47

Rodin takes Rose Pompon to Faringhea.

Scene 48

Morok's dressing room.

Over his armour Morok wears wide red trousers held at the ankles by gilt copper rings.

His kaftan is gold, black and purple.

At a table sits Couche-tout-nu.

Hollow cheeks.

Dull eyes.

MOROK: Your health, my boy.

COUCHE: Go to the devil.

MOROK: I am an angel. Got you out of prison.

COUCHE: Why?

MOROK: I have a good heart.

COUCHE: Oh yes. A thousand francs on condition I don't see Cephyse again.

MOROK: A man who is besotted by his mistress is no longer a man. Have some more brandy.

COUCHE: When I no longer think of her, I shall be dead.

GOLIATH: They're getting impatient, master.

MOROK: Good.

GOLIATH: La Mort is in one of her fits of rage. Like the night she killed that old horse.

MOROK: There is much pleasure in braving death before a terrified crowd. I am ready.

Scene 49

The famous black panther.

La Mort.

A fight to the death.

All Paris is here.

Elegant women.

Fill the boxes.

The stalls are full of young men.

A bigger audience than Racine gets.

What is the howling of an actor compared to the roaring of a lion?

Is that panther safe?

What if its chain breaks?

Enjoy it while you can.

The cholera will empty all the theatres.

He's coming from the north, with his walking stick under his arm.

Don't be so boring.

Look over there.

Mlle de Cardoville.

Isn't she lovely?

Exquisite.

Wit, money and freedom.

She lives in an enchanted palace.

Her bathroom is the talk of Paris.

Look at her bouquet.

Gardenias, purple hibiscus, amaryllis.

Who's that in the box opposite?

Faringhea.

An orange silk robe.

Bound with a green sash.

His black eyes sparkle.

A young man.

A white cashmere robe.

A scarlet turban.

A glittering dagger in his sash.

Djalma.

A girl.

A dress of white silk with cherry-coloured stripes.

Very low cut.

An enormous bouquet of roses.

Rose Pompon.

She beats time to the music.

A gigantic Indian forest.

Exotic trees.

Rocks.

A tropical sky.

A gloomy cave.

Look.

She leans towards him.

She is very fond of him.

What a handsome fellow.

Like a work of art.

Her hand is on his shoulder.

ROSE POMPON: That woman is staring at us.

DJALMA: It is Mlle de Cardoville.

FARINGHEA: Take the flowers and raise them to your lips. Did you see, my lord, how she shivers with jealousy?

ROSE POMPON: Come, Prince, give me back my bouquet.

The footlights dim.

A roar.

A second roar.

Deep growls like distant thunder drown the roar of the panther.

A lion and a tiger answer her from their dens at the back of the stage.

Morok carries a bow and a quiver of arrows.

La Mort appears.

Flat head lit by two flaming yellow eyes.

La Mort roars, showing two rows of fangs.

Djalma's eyes sparkle like black diamonds.

Morok places an arrow to the string of his bow.

He kneels behind a rock.

He takes aim.

The arrow hisses across the stage.

La Mort howls.

Applause.

Morok throws away the bow, and draws a dagger from his belt.

He takes it between his teeth and begins to crawl forward on his hands and knees.

Silence.

La Mort growls.

Morok rushes towards the panther.

La Mort throws herself upon him.

Adrienne's bouquet falls onto the stage.

Djalma bounds onto the stage, draws his dagger and rushes into the cave.

Morok is wounded.

La Mort tries to break her chain.

She rises onto her hind legs.

Djalma throws himself on his knees, plunges his dagger into her belly.

La Mort falls.

Djalma rises, pale, bleeding, wounded.

He holds Adrienne's bouquet.

Scene 50

Moon.

Stars.

A cheerless sky.

An icy north wind.

Montmartre.

Paris.

JOSEPH: The lights of a thousand fires light up the capital.

HERODIAS: The city is spread beneath our feet.

JOSEPH: When I touched the soil of France, the cholera's damp and icy hand was no longer clasped in mine.

HERODIAS: Perhaps the anger of the Lord is appeased. Perhaps the Lord will have pity, for your six descendants have met.

JOSEPH: Oh Lord, lay aside Thy wrath, I beseech thee, let me no longer be the instrument of Thy vengeance.

HERODIAS: Oh, that our suffering might cease.

JOSEPH: And the slavery of men who toil without rest, without recompense or hope.

HERODIAS: And the suffering of women who lie beneath the same yoke of slavery.

JOSEPH: Lord, dost thou not hear the sigh that rises from the earth?

HERODIAS: Joseph. The cholera. The spectre is with you again.

JOSEPH: The cholera's icy hand has hold of mine. Have mercy. Must I carry the plague into the city?

HERODIAS: We must go on.

JOSEPH: I can see the city walls.

HERODIAS: There is the city gate.

JOSEPH: Let not the sleeping town wake to cries of terror. Lord, there is yet time.

Scene 51

A large round table.

Covered with crimson velvet.

Silver plates piled with sandwiches.

Carp and anchovy butter.

Pickled tuna fish and truffles.

Crayfish tails in cream.

Crisp, golden pastry.

Delicious oyster pâtés.

Stewed in Madeira.

Flavoured with spiced sturgeon.

Pineapple biscuits.

Strawberry creams.

Wines from Bordeaux, Madeira and Alicante.

Sparkling like rubies and topazes in crystal decanters.

PRINCESS: Mme Grivois, is there a cushion for His Eminence to rest his feet?

GRIVOIS: Yes, Madame.

PRINCESS: And fetch some more wood for the fire.

GRIVOIS: Madame, it is already a furnace.

PRINCESS: We are taught self-sacrifice and mortification.

GRIVOIS: Just as you please, Madame.

Catholic delicacies.

Sacerdotal mitres made from burnt almonds.

A cardinal's hat out of cherries.

Ornamented with bands of caramel.

A superb crucifix in angelica.

ABBE: Cardinal Malipieri.

PRINCESS: Welcome, Cardinal Malipieri.

ABBE: Our meeting is, of course, in the strictest confidence.

CARDINAL: Some things are best kept secret, Princess.

PRINCESS: Indeed. Would Your Eminence like a hot water bottle?

CARDINAL: Not just at the moment.

PRINCESS: Will your Lordship take some refreshment? Some hot oyster páte?

CARDINAL: I cannot resist. And a little claret, if you please.

PRINCESS: Allow me.

CARDINAL: The church is indebted to you for the salutary direction you give to your religious institutions. Those crayfish tails look delicious. The pious should never go hungry.

ABBE: Perhaps it does the lower clergy no harm to go hungry. Unless they are carefully watched, they have a tendency to become infected with Gallic greed and rebel against the bishops.

CARDINAL: That is no problem as long as the bishops remember that they are Romans before they are Frenchmen.

ABBE: I hear that some of the lower clergy wish the French church to break with Rome completely. Indeed, the Abbé Gabriel de Rennepont has become the centre of such a movement.

CARDINAL: A dangerous young man. A Catholic Luther.

PRINCESS: A glass of Madeira?

ABBE: The Abbé Gabriel performed the final rites for a parishioner who committed suicide.

CARDINAL: Dear me. Is there any more cake?

ABBE: And he refused a set of silver gilt sacramental vessels with which one of the faithful wished to endow his parish.

CARDINAL: This young priest is most dangerous.

PRINCESS: Some strawberry cream, Your Eminence?

ABBE: His reverence Father Rodin thinks that if Your Eminence were to offer the Abbé Gabriel some eminent position in Rome, we might succeed in arousing in him some sentiments of ambition which have hitherto lain dormant.

CARDINAL: An excellent idea. With his evangelical powers, the Abbé Gabriel may rise very high if he is docile. Tell me, what do you think of Father Rodin?

ABBE: Your Eminence knows his abilities.

CARDINAL: I know he has replaced you. But can one have full confidence in him?

ABBE: He is not easy to understand.

CARDINAL: Is he ambitious for himself?

ABBE: What does Your Eminence think?

CARDINAL: I think that if his devotion to the Company concealed some personal ambition, it would be as well to discover it, for with the influence he has obtained at Rome he might shortly become most formidable.

ABBE: I agree with you.

CARDINAL: We must talk further.

Rodin, badly dressed as ever, enters, leaving muddy tracks on the soft carpet.

CARDINAL: We were just speaking of your reverence, my dear Father.

PRINCESS: Will you take something, my good Father?

RODIN: Thank you, Madame, I have already eaten my radish this morning.

CARDINAL: I have heard much about your reverence's frugality.

RODIN: Let us get down to business.

CARDINAL: M. Rodin, I have been sent from Rome to bring back news of the Rennepont affair.

ABBE: The Company is at your disposal.

CARDINAL: The interests of the Company are the interests of Rome.

ABBE: Your Eminence, the Reverend Father Rodin and I had some differences of opinion as to how the Rennepont affair should be conducted. As Your Eminence will be reporting back to our superior, I would ask you to listen to one or two questions I wish to put to Father Rodin.

RODIN: What is the point of these questions?

ABBE: Not to justify myself, but to clarify things for His Eminence.

RODIN: Speak then. But be quick.

ABBE: I will be as brief as possible. When Your Reverence thought fit to take my place, the Rennepont affair had taken a turn for the worse.

RODIN: You ordered me to write to Rome to bid them renounce all hope.

ABBE: That is true.

RODIN: We were faced with a desperate case given up by the best doctors. I undertook to bring it back to life. You used vulgar, military tactics. I have acted subtly. I have talked of liberty, progress and the emancipation of women with a hysterical girl, of love with a young tiger, of Bonapartish idolatory with a senile soldier, of Imperial glory and the humiliation of France with a stupid Marshal of France. Is it not a fine spectacle to see a spider obstinately weaving its net? To see the ugly little black animal crossing thread upon thread, fastening here, strengthening there, lengthening somewhere else. Return two hours later, and what will you find? The little black animal eating its kill, and in its web a dozen of the foolish flies bound so securely that the little black animal has only to choose the hour and moment of its repast.

ABBE: I do not dispute the intricacy of your plotting.

RODIN: Look into my spider's web and you will see that beautiful and insolent young girl, so proud six weeks ago, now pale, trembling, mortally wounded.

PRINCESS: The whole of Paris is talking about the Prince's ridiculous chivalrous act.

ABBE: Surely that will have reassured Mlle de Cardoville?

RODIN: I do not believe that killing black panthers proves one is a faithful lover.

CARDINAL: How does this affect the Rennepont affair?

RODIN: Adrienne de Cardoville is obsessed with the Prince, and will abandon the field of battle.

ABBE: She may cease to plot against us, but heartache will not prevent her from inheriting the money.

RODIN: I am thirsty. May I have a glass of claret?

PRINCESS: But of course, M. Rodin.

RODIN: It is very cold in here. Thank you. Let me continue. Prince Djalma is equally debilitated by his passion.

ABBE: And Marshal Simon, our military hero?

RODIN: I have written him unsigned letters, defiling his military record, and blaming you for the rumours.

ABBE: Blaming me?

Rodin presses his hand to his forehead.

PRINCESS: What is the matter?

RODIN: A slight headache. It will pass.

PRINCESS: Your eyes are bloodshot, my good Father.

RODIN: Do I read pity on your faces? Pity for this family of renegades whose ancestor, a relapsed heretic, not content with robbing us of our property, rises from his tomb a century and a half later?

He shudders. He fills his glass with wine.

CARDINAL: There is nothing in what you have done contrary to natural justice.

RODIN: I am like an alchemist who bends over the crucible which may give him either treasures or certain death –

He presses both hands to his forehead.

Stifles a cry of pain.

ABBE: What is the matter.

RODIN: I am giddy.

PRINCESS: Sit down.

RODIN: It is fatigue.

CARDINAL: My good Father, you are unwell.

His legs give way.

RODIN: It is so cold.

CARDINAL: Come nearer the fire.

PRINCESS: Dr Baleinier will be here directly.

Rodin utters a piercing cry.

He throws himself back convulsively.

He presses his two hands to his chest.

His hollow eyes are filled with blood.

His eyes are like two points of fire.

Convulsions draw the flabby damp skin tight over his bony cheekbones.

RODIN: I am burning.

He twists the buttons of his waistcoat and tears his filthy shirt front.

He tears his naked chest with his nails.

ABBE: We must restrain him.

Rodin seizes the Cardinal.

RODIN: Cardinal Malipieri. Someone in Rome suspects me.

CARDINAL: What are you saying?

RODIN: I have been poisoned.

PRINCESS: Ah, Dr Baleinier. Come in, come in. Father Rodin has had some kind of fit.

DOCTOR: Let me see.

CARDINAL: He thinks himself poisoned. Do you know anything about this, M. l'Abbé?

PRINCESS: What is it, Doctor?

DOCTOR: It is serious.

CARDINAL: What is it?

ABBE: What is it?

The Doctor draws back.

DOCTOR: It is the cholera.

They rush to the door.

Gabriel opens it from outside.

CARDINAL: Do not go in. He is dying of the cholera.

ABBE: We must leave at once.

CARDINAL: M. l'Abbé, we must talk again soon.

Gabriel runs towards Rodin.

Rodin is stretched upon the carpet, his limbs twisted with fearful cramps, writhing in pain.

RODIN: They are leaving me to die like a dog, the cowards. Help, help, someone.

GABRIEL: I am here, Father, to help you, to pray for you, if God calls you to him.

RODIN: Gabriel, forgive me for the evil I have done you. Do not leave me. Do not –

He falls back.

Scene 52

The cholera has arrived in Paris.

First case diagnosed.

At the Hotel de St. Dizier, Rue de Babylone.

Scene 53

A funeral pall spreads over Paris.

People leave their families in health, happiness.

Two hours later –

they find agony, death and despair.

Carts filled with coffins.

Everywhere the deafening sound of hammers.

Coffins nailed down.

Carts.

Drays.

Hackney coaches.

Swell the funeral procession.

The chanting of prayers replaces the chatter of the ballroom.

Tapers replace candles.

Revelry in the churchyards.

The sun sheds golden rays on the blackened sculptures of the porch of Notre Dame.

The cathedral square is full of the sick and the dying on their way to the nearby hospital.

Distant trumpets announce the Masquerade of the Cholera.

Led by a chariot, escorted by men and women on horseback, in elegant fancy dress.

Artists.

Young men about town.

Students.

Fall in with litters loaded with the dying.

Carriages filled with the dead.

To hell with Good Man Cholera.

Breakfast on one side of town.

Dinner on the other.

Scene 54

The tavern.

The great dining-room.

Drink, laugh, gamble and make love.

More wine.

MOROK: I am Bacchus, God of wine.

A swollen paunch.

An ivy crown.

A panther's skin.

A goblet festooned with flowers.

COUCHE: I am Good Man Cholera.

Green cardboard mask.

Red eyes.

A deathshead grin.

Down with the cholera.

Laugh and be merry.

Collar the cholera.

Long live the cholera.

COUCHE: My guts are on fire.

MOROK: A toast to the cholera!

The end of the world.

Turn the world upside-down.

We don't care.

COUCHE: Cephyse – Cephyse –

MOROK: More wine?

COUCHE: I am burning.

MOROK: Have some brandy.

COUCHE: I don't want any brandy.

MOROK: Well, perhaps you are right. A bottle of brandy is as dangerous as the barrel of a loaded pistol.

COUCHE: You think that I won't drink brandy because I am a coward?

MOROK: We've all shown our courage and defiance today. After all, you have played Good Man Cholera himself. Enough is enough.

COUCHE: Two bottles of brandy and two glasses.

MOROK: Why two?

COUCHE: For a duel.

A duel.

Bravo.

A fight to the death.

MOROK: You hear that, Jacques?

COUCHE: Waiter. Are you deaf?

The sun has set.

A hundred guests.

Dark corners.

Lit by lurid blues and greens.

From flaming cauldrons of punch.

Choose your weapon.

COUCHE: Look at us feasting with cholera patients. Such fine blues and greens.

MOROK: Are you ready?

COUCHE: Yes.

Morok's hand is steady.

Couche's hand trembles.

COUCHE: Drink from the bottle.

Morok raises the bottle to his lips.

Couche lowers the bottle.

Morok continues drinking.

COUCHE: My guts are burning.

His head falls back.

His neck is rigid.

He writhes.

MOROK: It is nothing.

Cephyse.

Hair in disorder.

Hollow cheeks.

Sunken eyes.

Clothed in rags.

CEPHYSE: Jacques, Jacques. It is I, Cephyse.

Cephyse covers his hands with kisses and tears.

COUCHE: Cephyse?

CEPHYSE: Yes, it is I.

COUCHE: Forgive me, Cephyse. Now I can die happy.

CEPHYSE: Thou shalt not die, Jacques.

COUCHE: I've got live coals in my stomach.

CEPHYSE: Have you made him drink brandy?

MOROK: He drank of his own free will.

COUCHE: You have been digging my grave.

CEPHYSE: Jacques, do not talk like that. You devil, you are killing him. Send for help.

MOROK: All the doctors are busy.

CEPHYSE: Then we must carry him to the hospital. Help me.

Jacques Rennepont dies in her arms.

Scene 55

A holy hotel.

Retreat for the devout.

An excellent cuisine.

A cosy chapel.

Food for body and spirit.

Here you may eat flesh on Fridays by special dispensation from Rome.

Three priests.

Two fat –

– one thin –

walk in the gardens.

Walking in pairs is not allowed.

PRIEST THREE: Look. His Eminence Cardinal Malipieri.

PRIEST TWO: On his daily visit to the Reverend Father Rodin.

PRIEST ONE: Sniffing from his little bottle of camphor, as usual. The cholera wouldn't dare go near him.

Scene 56

A fire.

Rags.

A mustard poultice.

Linen bandages.

A filthy nightcap.

A dirty pillow.

Rodin's eyes are closed.

His face is gaunt.

The skin clings to the bone.

His neck muscles stand out like cords

CARDINAL: How is the patient, Doctor?

DOCTOR: The fever is still raging in him. We may have to perform a painful operation.

CARDINAL: Have you sent for his confessor?

DOCTOR: M. Rodin refuses to make his confession.

CARDINAL: The Reverend Father's end must be Christian and exemplary. We shall embalm him and he must lie in state with six hundred tapers.

DOCTOR: Sir, the cholera laws do not allow such an exhibition.

CARDINAL: The cholera laws? Rome has her own laws. Has he been delirious again?

DOCTOR: Yes, he has.

CARDINAL: What has he said?

DOCTOR: Nothing coherent.

CARDINAL: Damnation. I shall have to speak to him myself.

DOCTOR: Cardinal – he is very weak.

CARDINAL: Then he will appreciate my spiritual guidance. My dear Father. How are you today? It is I, Reverend Father. Cardinal Malipieri.

DOCTOR: Please –

RODIN: You are very anxious to see me embalmed.

CARDINAL: After a life so well employed, it would be sweet to see you as an object of adoration for the faithful.

RODIN: If you do not leave me alone, I shall die in anything but a Christian manner.

He wipes his cracked, bleeding lips on an old cotton handkerchief.

CARDINAL: Be calm, my dear Father.

RODIN: My chest is on fire.

CARDINAL: Father. During your delirium Providence enabled you to make some important revelations.

RODIN: What revelations?

CARDINAL: It would be in your best interests to tell me everything. For the salvation of your soul, you must make the fullest confession about your intrigues with Rome.

RODIN: What intrigues?

CARDINAL: The intrigues you revealed during your delirium.

RODIN: If you have already heard them, there is no need for me to repeat them.

CARDINAL: Death is at hand. Do not die with a lie on your lips.

ABBE: I have news, Father Rodin.

RODIN: Good news may yet save me.

ABBE: Couche-tout-nu, one of the Rennepont heirs, died at an orgy three days ago.

RODIN: His death certificate will be worth forty millions to the Company of Jesus. What else?

ABBE: Your Reverence is in no condition to be burdened with worries.

RODIN: Tell me.

ABBE: Florine has died of the cholera. Mlle de Cardoville has held several meetings with the Marshal, the Abbé Gabriel and Agricola.

Rodin springs from the bed, dragging the sheets like a shroud around him.

His naked feet leave moist prints on the stone.

He writes.

ABBE: Father, this is madness.

CARDINAL: Another Lazarus.

ABBE: This letter is full of reason.

DOCTOR: What is happening? Your Reverence. Is he delirious again?

ABBE: His voice has gone.

DOCTOR: His skin is soft, almost moist. His pulse. Oh dear. We must perform the operation without delay.

ABBE: Are you sure?

DOCTOR: There is no choice. Your Reverence, the operation will be horribly painful. You must lie down.

Rodin hands a letter to the Abbé.

DOCTOR: Lean on me. Reverend Father, will you act as one of my assistants?

ABBE: No – I cannot. Some of our other priests will assist you.

CARDINAL: If he dies, will there be time to administer the sacraments in public?

DOCTOR: His agony may last a quarter of an hour.

CARDINAL: Well. We must be satisfied with that.

The three Jesuits.

DOCTOR: Reverend Fathers, I thank you for your help.

They bow as one.

DOCTOR: Draw near, gentlemen. This is the apparatus. Four steel trivets, each two inches in diameter and three in height. The centre of each trivet is filled with cotton wool. The instrument is held in the left hand by a wooden handle. In your right hand, you will each hold a small tube, eighteen inches long. At one end is an opening, the other end is splayed, to cover the trivet. Approach the patient, two on each side. Now, gentlemen, light the cotton wool. Place the trivet with the burning cotton wool on His Reverence's chest. Cover the trivet with the broad part of the tube, and then blow through the other end, to keep the fire burning. The operation is finished when all the layers of the skin have been burnt through.

Rodin writhes like a serpent, unable to cry out.

DOCTOR: Do not let him throw off the trivets. Courage, my dear Father, offer these sufferings to the Lord.

The sickening odour of burnt flesh.

A slight crackling.

Rodin's skin splits open.

Sweat pours.

DOCTOR: We must not stop now, or it will be all the more painful when we begin again. The fire has reached the deepest layer of skin. We are nearly there. Blow harder.

After a violent spasm.

Rodin lets out a cry of terrible pain, free, loud, sonorous.

DOCTOR: The chest is free, the lungs are working, his voice has returned, he is saved. Blow, gentlemen, blow. And you, my dear Reverend Father, shout as much as you please.

ABBE: I declare this is a miracle.

The last shreds of cotton wool are burnt through.

The priests remove the trivets.

Four large round burns. The skin is still smoking, the raw flesh visible beneath.

Rodin smiles.

He counts the wounds, touching them with his dirty nails.

RODIN: One Rennepont, two Renneponts, three Renneponts, four Renneponts. The heretics will be reduced to ashes, like the fragments of my flesh.

Scene 57

Cephyse.

Tangled hair.

Naked legs and feet.

An old, patched petticoat.

La Mayeux sits on a mattress.

Her elbows on her knees.

Her face in her thin white hands.

CEPHYSE: I have everything we need.

MAYEUX: Cephyse, art thou sure?

CEPHYSE: Quite sure.

MAYEUX: I have no reason to love life. But thou needst not die, because I have decided to.

CEPHYSE: I have always been idle, and sinful, while thou hast been industrious and good. Thou art an angel on earth. We shall die together.

MAYEUX: Agricola no longer needs me.

CEPHYSE: I cannot live without Jacques.

MAYEUX: How calm we are.

CEPHYSE: We are calm because we are resolved.

MAYEUX: Quite resolved.

They embrace.

CEPHYSE: To love one another so, and to part.

MAYEUX: To part, sister, Oh no. A better world awaits us. God cannot mean his creatures to be miserable for ever. It is getting late. Let us make haste.

CEPHYSE: Close the door and the window, and I shall light the charcoal.

MAYEUX: I'll twist the straw from our mattress to stop the holes in the roof.

CEPHYSE: No more draughts. We are as delicate as the rich.

MAYEUX: Now for the stove.

CEPHYSE: The fire is my business.

MAYEUX: But Cephyse –

CEPHYSE: Thou knowst the smell of charcoal gives thee a headache. Why suffer sooner than thou needst? Lie down.

MAYEUX: Do not be long, Cephyse.

CEPHYSE: In five minutes it will be over.

The garret grows dark.

Cephyse blows the fire.

The charcoal crackles.

CEPHYSE: Lie with thy head on my lap. Give me thy hand.

MAYEUX: I cannot see thee.

CEPHYSE: It will be as well not to see each other suffer.

MAYEUX: Thou art right.

CEPHYSE: I kiss your beautiful hair for the last time.

MAYEUX: I feel dizzy.

CEPHYSE: I am a little faint. But not dizzy. I am slower than thou to feel the effect of the charcoal.

MAYEUX: I was always ahead of thee at school.

CEPHYSE: I shall catch up with thee this time.

MAYEUX: My eyelids are heavy. I am numb. I have no pain.

CEPHYSE: I am giddy, Magdalene.

MAYEUX: It is not so difficult to die.

CEPHYSE: I cannot breathe.

MAYEUX: Cephyse help me.

CEPHYSE: Mayeux.

MAYEUX: Hold me.

Scene 58

Black clouds.

Masking the pale lustre of the moon.

CARDINAL: Does he trust you?

FARINGHEA: He does.

CARDINAL: Good. Continue to maintain his confidence.

FARINGHEA: I admire and respect this man who is stronger than the strongest.

CARDINAL: Man should be the obedient slave of the god he chooses.

FARINGHEA: As long as the god remains a god.

CARDINAL: You are a very religious man, in your own way.

FARINGHEA: When can I speak to him, my lord?

CARDINAL: In two or three days. He needs time to recover. Remember your instructions.

Scene 59

Rose Pompon has run upstairs.

Her shawl has slid down to her waist.

ROSE: Mademoiselle – my name is Rose Pompon. I must talk to you.

ADRIENNE: What on earth can someone in so immodest a dress have to say to me?

ROSE: Prince Djalma.

ADRIENNE: I see.

ROSE: I was at the theatre with him the night he killed the panther. I saw you there.

ADRIENNE: What do you want?

ROSE: I have left the Prince, Mademoiselle.

ADRIENNE: You have left him?

ROSE: Of my own accord, mind. Do not flatter yourself that I was unhappy. My prince would have married me. Does that hurt you?

ADRIENNE: Why do you hate me, Mademoiselle?

ROSE: Bless me, Mademoiselle, don't pretend you don't know. People don't rush to grab bouquets from the jaws of a panther for people they dislike, do they? I mean, in India the definition of politeness may include killing wild animals, but that isn't what we're used to in Paris. He was so handsome. I could see that he valued purity, and I thought, if I stay good, in the end he'll be unable to resist me. I've never been so good.

ADRIENNE: Do you regret having been virtuous?

ROSE: I wish I'd at least have had the pleasure of saying no.

ADRIENNE: Why did you stay with him?

ROSE: I got quite fond of him. He would have loved me, you know, if he hadn't been head over heels in love with you. He sits up all night, weeping.

ADRIENNE: I am sorry if you have been hurt, Mademoiselle.

ROSE: At first I was furious, then it brought tears to my eyes. If he isn't going to love me, then at least he may as well be happy. Mademoiselle, please take pity on him?

ADRIENNE: I will write to him. Thank you for coming to see me, my dear. Now I look more closely, that dress is really most becoming.

Scene 60

Djalma presses a letter to his lips.

FARINGHEA: My lord, do you perhaps owe your happiness to Mlle de Cardoville? Did I not tell you it would be so?

DJALMA: Yes, thou didst tell me.

FARINGHEA: Only yesterday you suffered cruelly. But you were not alone. This proud young girl suffered also. What must she have felt when she saw you at the theatre with another woman?

DJALMA: I cannot imagine. But I do not need to imagine. I shall know soon enough.

FARINGHEA: How do you mean, my lord?

DJALMA: I mean that in an hour I shall be with Mlle de Cardoville.

FARINGHEA: Indeed, my lord. Take care how you approach her!

DJALMA: I shall be myself.

FARINGHEA: This is a serious matter, my lord. Remember that women despise the love of he who asks humbly for what he might have by force.

DJALMA: Why advise me to use violence towards an angel of purity?

FARINGHEA: My lord, Parisian women cannot be trusted.

DJALMA: Yesterday I would have killed thee for less. But today, happy love renders me merciful. Thou must have met with little gentleness in thy life. In our country they charm serpents and tame the wildest tigers. I can tame thee. On the day I learned that my angel loved me, my happiness was great indeed, for in the morning I had an enemy, and by night he was a friend. Take my hand, Faringhea.

Scene 61

Gilded doors turn on their hinges.

Prince Djalma and Adrienne de Cardoville are alone together.

Scene 62

PRINCESS: My dear Father Rodin. I heard about the miracle.

RODIN: Miracle?

PRINCESS: Your recovery.

ABBE: Indeed, your courage was remarkable, M. Rodin.

RODIN: We must not waste time congratulating ourselves on the past. The first of June is approaching, and we have lost valuable time. Now. The letters to the Simon family.

ABBE: Sir – these letters to Marshal Simon – why do you think it is necessary to excite Marshal Simon's anger against me?

RODIN: It is absolutely essential. The letters suggest that you are the source of all the rumours; they rekindle his hatred of you; and they mock him because your holy vows protect you from his vengeance. He will be driven mad.

ABBE: What if the Marshal seeks me out?

RODIN: Are you afraid of him?

ABBE: I should be afraid of forgetting that I am a priest and of remembering too well that I was once a soldier.

RODIN: Still haunted by petty-minded matters of honour. If this brawling swordsman attacks you, would it really require a great effort to remain calm?

ABBE: I dare not speculate on such a question.

RODIN: And if the Marshal were to strike you?

ABBE: Enough.

RODIN: If Marshal Simon left the imprint of his hand on your cheek –

ABBE: Sir –

RODIN: There are no sirs here. We are only priests.

ABBE: If I were to be exposed to such an insult, I would pray heaven to give me resignation and humility.

RODIN: And no doubt heaven would hear your prayers. Now, we have more urgent matters to discuss.

PRINCESS: My niece, and the Prince.

RODIN: Indeed. The pagans are as bright and unchanging as a diamond in their happiness.

PRINCESS: What can we do?

RODIN: Give them time to inflame their base desires. I shall strike when I am ready, with Faringhea's help. We must send Gabriel to work in the cholera hospitals. He can save plenty of souls there if he survives.

ABBE: Surely your plan with the Simon family will have its limits. What if there were a reconciliation between father and daughters in spite of us?

RODIN: A good point, M. l'Abbé. In that case we would have to intervene.

ABBE: We could not make direct contact with them. They know us.

RODIN: Indeed. But there is someone here who is not known to them.

PRINCESS: But of course, Father. The girls do not know me.

Scene 63

BLANCHE: Sister, of what art thou thinking?

ROSE: Of Paris, the golden city of our dreams. What has become of it?

BLANCHE: It is a place of tears.

ROSE: I dreamed last night that the angel Gabriel came and took us from the earth.

BLANCHE: I too dreamed of Gabriel.

ROSE: He spread his beautiful white wings.

BLANCHE: And we smiled as he took us by the hand and carried us to the depths of the blue sky.

ROSE: Where our mother awaited us with open arms.

BLANCHE: Perhaps it is meant to be. If our father no longer loves us. He has not been to see us for two days.

ROSE: Do you believe the letters? 'Your father is miserable and you are the cause of his distress.'

BLANCHE: 'Spare him those signs of tenderness which give him so much more pain than pleasure.'

ROSE: 'Each caress is a dagger. Cultivate reserve and you will alleviate his sorrow.'

BLANCHE: Perhaps we are not the children he dreamed of.

ROSE: His friends must have daughters who are beautiful and talented – like Mlle de Cardoville.

BLANCHE: We must be such a disappointment to him.

Scene 64

Marshal Simon paces.

SIMON: Who is the traitor who tells me that all my friends despise me and that my daughters hate me? I have fought with the sword for twenty-five years, and now I am to be tortured with the pen to gratify some unknown hate. D'Aigrigny is at the bottom of this. He has always been my enemy. I must finish with him, once and for all.

DAGOBERT: General, he is a priest. You cannot fight him.

SIMON: I must be avenged. Can you not understand? Even my children turn from me.

DAGOBERT: They think they have displeased their father.

SIMON: They love you better than they do me. For me they have only distant respect. I cannot bear it.

DAGOBERT: Of course they are more familiar with me. They have known me all their lives. You have been sad and pre-occupied. What you take for coldness is anxiety for you. You complain because they love you too much.

SIMON: Sir, enough.

DAGOBERT: Oh yes, it is enough. Why defend unfortunate children who can only love? General, I implore you. Let me call them.

DAGOBERT: For the first time in my life I shall disobey you. Rose. Blanche.

ROSE: Yes, Dagobert.

DAGOBERT: Come, children. Come. Do not be afraid. Your father wishes to see you.

SIMON: Good day, my children.

ROSE: Good day, Father.

SIMON: I was not able to see you yesterday.

BLANCHE: We were sorry.

SIMON: Are you angry with me for neglecting you?

BLANCHE: No, Father.

SIMON: Do you forgive me?

ROSE: Of course we do.

BLANCHE: How could we do otherwise?

ROSE: We love you, Father.

DAGOBERT: Did I not tell you?

SIMON: Thou wast a better father than myself, old friend. Come and embrace them. I shall not be jealous any more.

Scene 65

The ruins of an abbey.

A pine forest.

Ivy.

Moss.

Stones.

Black with age.

A statue.

A headless human figure.

In its hand a plate.

On the plate a head.

St John the Baptist.

Put to death by order of Herodias.

HERODIAS: I walk with difficulty. My feet bleed. I feel pain. I have a burning thirst. I see the stream, I throw myself on my knees to quench my thirst in the crystal current. In this mirror I see that I have grown old. Perhaps I may hope to die. If the wrath of heaven is now appeased, let justice prevail on earth for all.

Wind in the pine trees.

The silver disc of the moon.

A crucifix.

A figure on the cross.

JOSEPH: My hair has turned grey. I am growing old. Oh Lord, hast thou finally pardoned me? If the wrath of heaven is now appeased, let justice prevail on earth for all.

Scene 66

BLANCHE: I have combed your hair.

ROSE: And now I shall do the same for you.

BLANCHE: We are really happy, Dagobert.

DAGOBERT: That's how I like to see you.

PRINCESS: I believe I have the honour of speaking to Marshal Simon's gracious daughters?

DAGOBERT: Yes, Madame.

PRINCESS: He is a brilliant and generous man.

ROSE: We love him.

DAGOBERT: I am proud at the praise you bestow on the Marshal.

PRINCESS: I thought he would be receptive to an appeal for charity. I have come to you on behalf of the cholera victims.

ROSE: He is not here at the moment, Madame.

PRINCESS: Oh dear, that is a pity.

ROSE: We could help the victims of this terrible disease, could we not, Dagobert?

DAGOBERT: But of course. Madame, they are generous children.

BLANCHE: Thank you, Dagobert.

ROSE: We have no more tender and devoted friend than Dagobert, Madame.

PRINCESS: I can readily believe it, Mademoiselle.

DAGOBERT: Excuse me. I will fetch you something, Madame.

PRINCESS: Thank you.

ROSE: We only wish that we could do more.

PRINCESS: If you knew how many touching acts I witness every day. Only yesterday I was visiting a hospital near here. I saw a lady accompanied by two daughters, young, charming, charitable as you are. They offered to help nurse the patients. And in the same establishment I was struck by the sight of a young priest, or perhaps I should say, an angel, who was bringing the consolation of religion. Had you seen the Abbé Gabriel –

ROSE: The Abbé Gabriel?

PRINCESS: You know him, then?

BLANCHE: Oh yes, Madame. He is Dagobert's adopted son.

PRINCESS: The Abbé Gabriel was comforting the sick. And he spoke of the help of young women who might have the time and charity to help those less fortunate than themselves.

BLANCHE: Perhaps it is our duty to help.

PRINCESS: I knew the moment I saw you that your hearts would respond. On the other hand, perhaps the work would be too taxing for you.

BLANCHE: Oh no. We are strong.

ROSE: Dagobert will not let us go.

PRINCESS: Would M. Dagobert stop you performing your duty?

ROSE: He would be afraid for us.

PRINCESS: I have been visiting these hospitals. I have not felt the least symptom of the disease. It is not contagious.

ROSE: I do not know –

PRINCESS: You have had the misfortune to lose your mother, I believe?

ROSE: Alas, yes, Madame.

PRINCESS: She will survey you from Paradise – she did receive the last sacraments, of course?

BLANCHE: There was no priest near.

PRINCESS: Oh dear. Without the sacraments, her soul wanders through purgatory awaiting the Lord's mercy. But you must not despair, my children. She can attain everlasting bliss through your act of devotion to the Abbé Gabriel.

BLANCHE: Oh, Madame, you make everything so clear. Rose, we must tell Dagobert.

PRINCESS: No – say nothing to that excellent man. Think how delighted he will be when you return to tell him how your act of Christian charity will ensure your mother's salvation.

ROSE: We are grateful to you, Madame, for having thought of us.

Scene 67

Hospital orderlies.

ORDERLY ONE: Look over there.

ORDERLY TWO: Two girls, dressed in mourning. Relatives of one of the dead, no doubt.

ORDERLY ONE: May I help you, ladies?

ROSE: We have come to help the Abbé Gabriel.

BLANCHE: Do you know where he is?

ORDERLY ONE: Please. Look for yourselves.

A huge room.

Once a ballroom.

Now divided by partitions.

Four rows of beds.

ROSE: So many creatures writhing in agony. How they suffer.

BLANCHE: Oh, Rose. Take my hand.

ROSE: The cholera. Blanche.

BLANCHE: I remember our mother.

ROSE: I feel cold.

BLANCHE: It is only fear.

ROSE: You are right. Be careful, Blanche – what is the matter?

BLANCHE: My head hurts.

ROSE: It is only fear.

BLANCHE: I am dizzy.

ROSE: And I.

BLANCHE: Rose, how pale thou art.

ROSE: Like thee, sister.

BLANCHE: Dost thou feel cold?

ROSE: Yes. I cannot see.

BLANCHE: My chest is on fire.

ROSE: We are going to die.

BLANCHE: Together.

ROSE: Look. Gabriel.

GABRIEL: Great heavens.

ROSE: Sister, dost see the Archangel?

BLANCHE: Pray to God for our mother and for us.

ROSE: We did not think to die so soon.

GABRIEL: You must not die. Think of your father. He needs you.

BLANCHE: Tell our father that our last thought was of him.

GABRIEL: Does Dagobert know you are here?

ROSE: No. Do not let our father scold him.

GABRIEL: Almighty Father. Why should these children die this cruel death?

BLANCHE: Let us be buried together.

ROSE: Sister.

BLANCHE: Sister.

DAGOBERT: My children, my children.

Scene 68

RODIN: To Rome. Another two despatched. To Marshal Simon. Your daughters are dead. Who do you think is to blame? To Faringhea. Find the girl, Pompon.

Scene 69

Dark and stormy.

A lantern.

GRAVEDIGGER: Here it is.

SAMUEL: Are you sure?

GRAVEDIGGER: Of course. Look. Two bodies in one coffin.

SAMUEL: Alas.

GRAVEDIGGER: What else do you want?

SAMUEL: Here is more gold.

GRAVEDIGGER: Very well. Tomorrow night. Two o'clock.

SAMUEL: Mind you are punctual.

Scene 70

ADRIENNE: My love, we have had the courage to resist every temptation, and have proved that our love is pure. Now we must think about the future. Our love must be consecrated in the eyes of the world. And we must be equal in the eyes of God. Djalma, the day our hands are joined, what hymns of gratitude will ascend to heaven. I will find a noble spirit to join us. I love thee, Djalma.

DJALMA: Why should we wait, Adrienne?

ADRIENNE: Because our love must be consecrated by the benediction of heaven.

DJALMA: But are we not free?

ADRIENNE: Yes, yes, my love, we are free. Let us be worthy of our liberty.

DJALMA: Adrienne, mercy.

ADRIENNE: I ask thee also to have mercy on our love. Do not profane it. A few days longer.

DJALMA: Thine image follows me, thy breath burns me. I cannot sleep. To see thee every day – to desire thee like this –

ADRIENNE: Thou art so beautiful in thy passion. No. I must go.

DJALMA: Adrienne!

FARINGHEA: Oh, my lord, my lord.

DJALMA: What is wrong? Faringhea, what has happened?

FARINGHEA: Unhappy love, betrayed love, tears of blood.

DJALMA: Of what dost thou speak?

FARINGHEA: I speak of my love.

DJALMA: Thy love?

FARINGHEA: My lord. I have found a woman to respond to my passion. And now I have been shamefully betrayed.

DJALMA: I will console thee. Remember that I too once thought that she who is the angel of my life did not love me. What causes thy suspicions.

FARINGHEA: I learned today that she has made an appointment with a man she knew before she met me.

DJALMA: Perhaps this appointment has no guilt to it.

FARINGHEA: No, my lord. I should not have told you. It is from my dagger that I should ask counsel.

DJALMA: Faringhea, listen to me – It is not of thy knife that thou must take counsel, but of thy friend. Go to this meeting. But not alone. I shall come with thee.

FARINGHEA: You, my lord?

DJALMA: Perhaps I may save thee from a crime. I know the blindness of first rage.

FARINGHEA: And when I have killed, then I will kill myself. The dagger for the false ones, poison for me.

DJALMA: Faringhea –

FARINGHEA: Two or three drops of this poison from the hilt of my dagger and death comes slowly, peacefully, in a few hours without pain.

DJALMA: Give me the dagger.

FARINGHEA: No, my lord.

DJALMA: I would not force thee. Give it to me.

FARINGHEA: Here. I renounce my vengeance. But I must still know the truth. Are you ready, my lord?

DJALMA: I am ready.

FARINGHEA: Then we must delay no longer. Come.

Scene 71

Rodin paces.

Hands in his back pockets.

Head bowed.

He bites his nails.

He walks up and down.

He stops.

He stamps his foot.

He raises his eyes.

He scratches his head.

RODIN: Oh, the passions, the passions, what a magical instrument they form if you touch the keys with a skilful hand. The foolish think they have crushed us men of the church, when they say you take command of the spiritual – conscience, soul – and we keep the temporal. They forget that the mind and the soul govern the body, and the body is therefore ours too. Soon they will see what it is to have spirituality in the hands of a priest who for fifty years has lived frugally, chastely, and when he is Pope will continue to live frugally, chastely.

Father Caboccini, from Rome.

Plump, blind in one eye.

A smiling, rosy, joyous face, splendidly crowned with thick chestnut hair which curls like that of a wax doll.

Caboccini throws himself on Rodin and kisses him loudly on both cheeks.

Rodin tries to extricate himself from the Roman's exaggerated tenderness.

Caboccini's arms are strong.

His embraces are accompanied by the most affectionate exclamations.

Caboccini finally relinquishes his hold.

Rodin readjusts his dirty collar.

RODIN: Your humble servant, Father.

CABOCCINI: At last I see the superb light of our sacred Company. I salute you from my heart.

RODIN: Father, I am not a light. I am an obscure labourer in the Lord's vineyard.

CABOCCINI: You are right, Father. I prostrate myself before you.

RODIN: Please. This is mere idolatory, Father. Tell me the object of your journey.

CABOCCINI: The object, my dear Father, fills me with joy. The object transports, delights, enchants me.

RODIN: Well, what is it?

CABOCCINI: This note from our very reverend General will inform you, my dear Father.

He kisses it.

Delivers it to Rodin.

Rodin kisses it and opens it.

CABOCCINI: I shall be your secretary, your second self. I shall have the joy of being with you day and night.

Scene 72

FARINGHEA: In here, my lord.

DJALMA: It is dark.

FARINGHEA: Excuse me, my lord.

A door opens, closes and is locked.

DJALMA: Faringhea?

FARINGHEA: My lord. If I have tricked you into coming here, it is because the blindness of your passion would have prevented you from accompanying me. Watch and listen.

DJALMA: Faringhea. Faringhea, open the door.

FARINGHEA: Watch and listen.

Silence.

Darkness.

A faint light.

A divan with cushions.

A woman.

A hooded cloak.

She stands.

She walks towards the mirror.

She turns.

The cloak glides down to her feet.

Red-gold curls float over her naked shoulders.

It is Rose Pompon, dressed to look like Adrienne.

Her back is towards Djalma.

She loosens her hair.

She begins to unfasten her gown.

FARINGHEA: Watch her carefully, Prince Djalma. She is expecting her lover, Agricola Baudoin, the young poet.

Djalma draws his dagger.

Djalma bounds through the door.

He stabs Rose Pompon.

FARINGHEA: You are avenged. Come, my lord, we must hurry away.

Scene 73

DJALMA: It was my fault she did not love me. She concealed her indifference out of generosity. Nothing can bring her back. Not even my death.

He takes the phial.

He throws the dagger on the ermine carpet.

The white is stained with red.

DJALMA: Blood for blood. My life for hers. I drink.

A cry of alarm.

DJALMA: Adrienne.

ADRIENNE: Why art thou here?

DJALMA: God is kind and just.

ADRIENNE: Blood on the dagger.

DJALMA: Thou art here, beautiful, pure.

ADRIENNE: Has thou killed someone?

DJALMA: Thou art alive.

ADRIENNE: There is blood upon this dagger.

DJALMA: I threw it down when I took the poison. I thought I had killed thee and I came here to die.

ADRIENNE: Oh my God.

DJALMA: Here. The crystal phial.

Adrienne seizes the phial and drinks.

ADRIENNE: Thou hast killed and death must expiate thy crime. I will not survive thee. Why dost thou weep?

DJALMA: For thee, for thee.

ADRIENNE: No more tears, only smiles of love and joy. Our cruel enemies will not triumph. They wish to make us miserable. But our felicity shall be the envy of the world.

DJALMA: Adrienne.

ADRIENNE: Our death shall be celestial. This poison is slow. I adore thee, my Djalma.

DJALMA: I feel thy warm breath on my cheek. I see the flame that darts from thine eyes.

ADRIENNE: Oh my lover, my husband, how beautiful thou art. Those eyes, that brow, those lips, how I love them. Heaven wills that we should be united. Only this morning I gave a gift for the poor to the Abbé Gabriel, the apostolic man who was to bless our union. We have nothing to regret. Our mortal souls will pass away in a kiss and ascend, full of love to the God who is all love.

DJALMA: Adrienne.

ADRIENNE: Djalma.

The curtains fall over the nuptial and funeral couch.

Two hours later Adrienne and Djalma breathe their last sigh in voluptuous agony.

Scene 74

Marshal Simon.

His hair white.

Unshaven.

Two swords in his belt.

SIMON: My children are dead.

ABBE: Sir, listen to me.

SIMON: Your hate followed my wife into exile. You and your accomplices sent my children to certain death. For twenty years you have haunted me. We will fight to the death.

ABBE: Sir, you forget that my profession forbids me to fight.

SIMON: So a priest may commit any crime behind the shelter of his black gown? We shall see. I strike you, sir. Coward.

ABBE: You will have blood? Very well, then.

SIMON: At last.

ABBE: No. I am a minister of the Lord and must not shed blood.

He places the blade beneath his heel and breaks the weapon into two pieces.

Simon places his blade under his heel, breaks it in half, picks up the pointed end, wraps his black silk cravat round the broken part.

SIMON: We will fight with daggers.

ABBE: Like butchers, with knives?

SIMON: Must I spit on you to make the little blood you have left rise to your face? There, Judas.

The Abbé wraps a handkerchief round the blade.

They fight.

Marshal Simon is killed.

The Abbé is wounded.

RODIN: I always told you, my dear Father, that your old military habits would be the death of you.

ABBE: Before I die, I will unmask you.

RODIN: How fortunate that I am here. I can receive your last confession.

ABBE: May God have mercy on me. I have been a great sinner.

RODIN: And a great fool. He has breathed his last. It is the first of June.

Scene 75

CABOCCINI: I bring you greetings from His Excellency Cardinal Malipieri.

FARINGHEA: Thank you.

CABOCCINI: You know what to do?

FARINGHEA: Yes. Before leaving home, will Father Rodin go to pray in the chapel as usual?

CABOCCINI: I believe so.

FARINGHEA: It is possible that the Reverend Father might forget to go to the chapel. In that case, pray remind him of his pious duty.

CABOCCINI: I see that you take great interest in his salvation.

FARINGHEA: I do.

CABOCCINI: Continue in this way and you will belong to us completely.

Scene 76

Panes of coloured glass.

A font in sculptured marble.

A dark corner.

Faringhea kneels.

Footsteps.

Rodin dips his fingers into the font.

He kneels.

He rises.

He bows to the altar.

Faringhea bows.

Rodin dips his hand into the holy water.

Faringhea holds the brush which stands by the font.

Pressing the damp brush, Rodin wets his thumb and forefinger and traces the sign of the cross on his forehead.

Faringhea is alone.

He sinks down.

His face buried in his hands.

Father Caboccini watches.

Scene 77

SAMUEL: You represent the only remaining heir of the Rennepont family, the Abbé Gabriel de Rennepont?

RODIN: Yes, sir. I bear his power of attorney.

SAMUEL: The securities are contained in this casket. A total of two hundred and twelve million, one hundred and seventy-five thousand francs.

RODIN: I thought myself proof against all emotion.

CABOCCINI: My dear Father.

RODIN: I did not survive the cholera to die of joy on the 1st of June.

Caboccini draws a paper from his pocket and kisses it.

CABOCCINI: On receipt of the present order, the Reverend Father Rodin will deliver up all his powers to the Reverend Father Caboccini who will receive the Rennepont inheritance.

RODIN: What is the date on that document?

CABOCCINI: The 11th of May.

RODIN: I received this note last night from Rome, dated the 18th of May. I am named General of the Order. These millions must be delivered to me.

SAMUEL: Heaven will not allow this fortune to be a reward for falsehood, hypocrisy and murder.

RODIN: Murder, sir?

Curtains are drawn aside.

The bluish light of a silver lamp.

Five bodies dressed in long black robes lying on black biers.

Jacques Rennepont.

Rose and Blanche Simon.

Adrienne and Djalma.

SAMUEL: Behold those whom thou hast slain. As they fell, it was my responsibility to obtain their remains, that they may all repose in the same grave. Murderer.

RODIN: Come, sir, this is a waxwork exhibition. Let us finish our business.

SAMUEL: Since your infernal soul is incapable of remorse, perhaps it may be shaken by disappointed avarice.

RODIN: What are you doing?

SAMUEL: The spoils of your victims will escape your murderous hands. In a few minutes there will be nothing but ashes.

RODIN: Help. Water. Water.

SAMUEL: Nothing.

For the first time in his life Rodin weeps.

Suddenly, dreadful pains.

RODIN: The treasure may be destroyed, but I am still General of the Order.

CABOCCINI: What is it?

RODIN: If I did not live on roots – water – bread – I would think I had been poisoned.

The Princess.

Faringhea.

RODIN: Faringhea. Ah. You. The holy water. I am burning. Help me. Please help me, for God's sake.

FARINGHEA: I have obeyed the Cardinal. For me the Company has taken the place of Bohwanie. Glory to the Company. Glory.

Scene 78

GABRIEL: My dear Joseph. I am sitting by the window, looking out over the farmyard.

Dagobert sits under a pear tree.

Francoise by his side.

Agricola stands nearby.

GABRIEL: The family, resting at the end of the day. My heart rises to heaven.

FRANCOISE: My dear – thou art weeping.

DAGOBERT: It is nothing.

FRANCOISE: Come, tell me.

DAGOBERT: Today is the first of June. Look.

The medal.

GABRIEL: Before she died, Adrienne de Cardoville gave me a sum of money, with which I bought this farm. Agricola has become an excellent farmer, and even I have put my hand to the plough. Our enemies tried to convince us that we were born to suffer. But all is not pain and sorrow. God is the supreme essence of goodness and can take no delight in misery. Many people are hungry, cold and without shelter, in the midst of the riches that the Creator gave for the happiness of all. For did not He say: 'Love One Another'. Thank you for your letter, my dear Joseph. It is painful, but you must submit to the church's discipline, as I do. If they forbid you to see me or write to me, then so be it. I shall not write again. Pray for me. Farewell, my friend. Gabriel de Rennepont.

Scene 79

HERODIAS: A glimmer in the east.

JOSEPH: The stars still shine.

HERODIAS: Dawn is breaking. I can see the valley.

JOSEPH: The woods.

HERODIAS: The mountain.

JOSEPH: How many times have we witnessed the beginning of the day with grief?

HERODIAS: But what happiness now, as the Lord's mercy means that every day brings us nearer the grave.

JOSEPH: Soon Gabriel, too, will resign his immortal soul to God.

HERODIAS: The struggle has been hard and long, but it is over now.

JOSEPH: The sun is rising. Our last day on earth, my sister. My eyes grow dim.

HERODIAS: I am growing weaker. Eternal rest is at hand, Joseph.

JOSEPH: We are forgiven, Herodias.

The sun.

Radiant.

Dazzling.

The valley is flooded with light.

END